THIRD EDITION

Skills for Success

LISTENING AND SPEAKING

Robert Freire | Tamara Jones

OXFORD

UNIVERSITY PRESS

OXFORD
UNIVERSITY PRESS

198 Madison Avenue
New York, NY 10016 USA

Great Clarendon Street, Oxford, OX2 6DP, United Kingdom

Oxford University Press is a department of the University of Oxford.
It furthers the University's objective of excellence in research, scholarship,
and education by publishing worldwide. Oxford is a registered trade
mark of Oxford University Press in the UK and in certain other countries

ISBN: 978 0 19 490516 9   STUDENT BOOK 4 WITH IQ ONLINE PACK
ISBN: 978 0 19 490504 6   STUDENT BOOK 4 AS PACK COMPONENT
ISBN: 978 0 19 490540 4   IQ ONLINE STUDENT WEBSITE

Printed in China

This book is printed on paper from certified and well-managed sources

ACKNOWLEDGEMENTS

Back cover photograph: Oxford University Press building/David Fisher

*The author and publisher are grateful to those who have given permission to
reproduce the following extracts and adaptations of copyright material:*
p. 5 from "Leadership isn't just for the boss" by CBC Radio-Canada, 31 July
2017. © CBC Radio-Canada. Reproduced by permission; p. 11 Hammett,
Pete. "3 Ways to Break Out of Your Executive Bubble." Audio blog post.
Leading Effectively. Center for Creative Leadership, 2007. www.ccl.org.
Drawn from *Unbalanced Influence: Recognizing and Resolving the Impact of Myth
and Paradox in Executive Performance,* Davies-Black Publishing, Copyright
© 2007 Pete Hammett. Reproduced by permission; p. 35 from "Colour
Schemes: How Colours Make You Buy" from Under the Influence with
Terry O'Reilly, 10 May 2018, CBC Radio. © Terry O'Reilly. Reproduced by
permission; p. 62 from "A lament for the sad state of financial literacy
among young people" by CBC Radio-Canada, The Sunday Edition, 6 March
2016. © CBC Radio-Canada. Reproduced by permission; p. 154 adapted
from "The Power of Serendipity" from CBS News Sunday Morning, 7
October 2007. © CBS News. Reproduced by permission of CBS News
Archives; p. 180 from "Automation and Us" by CBC Radio-Canada, 5
October 2014, 6 March 2016. © CBC Radio-Canada. Reproduced by
permission.

Illustrations by: pp. 81, 82, 96, 99 Mark Duffin; p. 73 Joe Taylor.

*We would also like to thank the following for permission to reproduce the following
photographs:* **123rf:** pp. 5 (informal business meeting/Mark Bowden),
36 (BP logo/Alexandr Blinov), 57 (student/Antonio Diaz), 70 (parents
holding infant/Mark Bowden), 83 (kerosene lamp/Oleksandr Kozak), 104
(Peking duck/Mikhail Valeev), 105 (drone/Goce Risteski), 119 (chocolate
ice cream/Hans Geel), 155 (coffee beans/Ilja Generalov), 156 (GPS/Igor
Stevanovic), 173 (popsicles/Jennifer Barrow); **Alamy:** pp. 2 (conductor
and orchestra/imageBROKER), 11 (business meeting/MBI), 15 (colleagues
working together/Albert Shakirov), 16 (John Donahoe/ZUMA Press, Inc.),
18 (student listening to podcast/Dan Grytsku), 22 (supervisor giving talk
to employees/Hero Images Inc.), 30 (Agatha Christie/Everett Collection
Historical), 32 (boy in messy room/Big Cheese Photo LLC), 38 (Owens
Corning advertisement/Cal Sport Media), 49 (stressed woman/Andriy
Popov), 52 (woman voting/Hero Images Inc.), 54 (Seijin no Hi celebration/
dpa picture alliance), 62 (woman counting money/Hero Images Inc.), 78
(space rocket/Konstantin Shaklein), 104 (shark liver oil/BSIP SA), 108 (man
assembling drone/Montgomery Martin), 109 (organic sign/David Angel),
113 (family walking/Carmen K. Sisson/Cloudybright), 135 (intern and
supervisor/LightField Studios Inc.), 147 (women leaving college library/
Adam Bronkhorst), 152 (abseiling in cave/Cavan), 154 (doctor examining
x-ray/Blend Images), 156 (pacemaker/Phanie), (Velcro/Stocksnapper),
158 (magnetron/Aleksandr Volkov), 166 (brain injury/BSIP SA), (Phineas
Gage/ART Collection), (skull graphic/BSIP SA), 168 (nomad with camel/
Guillem Lopez), 170 (professor lecturing/Reeldeal Images), 172 (raised
hands/Wavebreak Media ltd), 176 (man photographing nature/Cultura
Creative RF), 177 (woman in deep sea submersible/SeaTops), 182 (doctor
and patient/Hero Images Inc.), 190 (traffic/Don Bartell), 201 (man with
personal assistant/Image navi - QxQ images), 203 (family on video call/
Tetra Images, LLC); **Getty:** pp. cover (prismatic background of binary
code/KTSDESIGN/SCIENCE PHOTO LIBRARY), 4 (woman with award/Hill
Street Studios), 6 (restaurant manager and employee/andresr), 8 (boss and
employee in shop/andresr), 13 (suggestion box/Randy Faris), 20 (female
speaker/Caiaimage/Martin Barraud), 25 (sports team coach/SolStock),
26 (modern workplace/Bloomberg), 45 (employee leaving work/Hero
Images), 51 (woman looking at notes/PeopleImages), 54 (Quinceañera/
Pixelchrome Inc), 55 (women in laundromat/Hero Images), 72 (graduates/
Â© Hiya Images/Corbis), 77 (man moving house/Matthias Ritzmann), 87
(circuit board/TimeStopper), 88 (Gordon Moore/Justin Sullivan), 89 (tech
items/Yuri_Arcurs), 94 (solar windows/Ashley Cooper), 101 (engineers
working on turbines/Westend61), 102 (man spraying crops/D-Keine), 107
(farmer with tablet/Ariel Skelley), 117 (scientists monitoring bananas/
chinaface), 123 (fat chicken/Suphanat Wongsanuphat), 125 (underwater
grown tomatoes/Alexis Rosenfeld), 126 (winter climbers /David Trood),
129 (colleagues chatting in office/Ezra Bailey), 130 (Scott Nash/The
Washington Post), (John Paul DeJoria/John M. Heller), (Michael Acton
Smith/Oli Scarff/Staff), 132 (woman looking at whiteboard/andresr), 134
(man and woman reviewing CVs/Hero Images), 136 (woman delivering
drinks/Paul Bradbury), 137 (woman in office/electravk), 139 (interns at tech
company/Anchiy), 141 (women shaking hands/laflor), 143 (friends in café/
ferrantraite), 145 (hand petting rhino/Suneet Bhardwaj), (woman walking
down steps/gradyreese), 151 (committee job interview/filadendron), 162
(twin babies/YinYang), 178 (miniature drone/Andre Dancer/EyeEm), 193
(car engineer/Monty Rakusen), 201 (woman hugging robot/NurPhoto),
(medical care robot/JIJI PRESS/Stringer); **OUP:** p. 35 (smiling woman);
Shutterstock: pp. 14 (employee at door/Dean Drobot), 28 (tidy work
desk/thodonal88), 35 (colorful ties/Fedor Selivanov), 36 (McDonalds sign/
Jonathan Weiss), (Tiffany box/AlesiaKan), (Easyjet airplane/NUI BLANCO),
(NYC taxi/elbud), (Apple logo/r.classen), (Starbucks logo/CHALERMPHON
SRISANG), (Louboutin shoes/andersphoto), 37 (pink insulation in house/
Rachid Jalayanadeja), 40 (waterfront promenade/Malgorzata Litkowska), 41
(messy work desk/Andrey_Popov), 46 (casually dressed man/Rido), (formal
dressed man/Bangkok Click Studio), 57 (teacher/Monkey Business Images),
60 (man thinking/Syda Productions), 64 (friends laughing/Monkey Business
Images), 66 (laptop/LightField Studios), 84 (waterwheel/nikolansfoto),
110 (large plate of fries/stockcreations), 112 (chocolates/Iakov Filimonov),
114 (ice cream sundae/stockcreations), 119 (strawberry ice cream/beats1),
122 (men in café/Sjale), 123 (ripe raspberries/Olexandr Panchenko),
(moldy raspberries/Andrzej Rostek), (slim chicken/Jakkrit Phomwong),
156 (cookies/Mouse family), (rechargeable batteries/art_photo_sib), (tea/
Arancio), 159 (lightbulb moment/Billion Photos), 161 (prehistoric cave
paintings/thipjang), 174 (Rosetta Stone/Claudio Divizia), 180 (factory with
robots/AlexLMX), (self-checkout/frantic00), (robot vacuum cleaner/Jtal),
(robot arm/THINK A), 183 (pilots in cockpit/Skycolors), 184 (automation
concept/PopTika), 187 (adult photographing scenery/ProStockStudio), 188
(driverless car/Snapic_PhotoProduction), 191 (smart home/zhu difeng), 193
(dentist and patient/Africa Studio), (dietician/Stasique), 194 (self-driving
truck/Tony Avelar/AP), 195 (3D printer/science photo), 198 (robot typing on
computer/Andrey_Popov), 200 (woman talking on phone/Antonio Guillem);
Third party: pp. 30 (Leon Heppel/Office of NIH History and Stetten
Museum, U.S. National Institutes of Health), 57 (Rachel Weinstein/Rachel
Weinstein/Adulting school), 80 (Hannah Herbst/Julie Herbst).

ACKNOWLEDGMENTS

We would like to acknowledge the teachers from all over the world who participated in the development process and review of *Q: Skills for Success* Third Edition.

USA

Kate Austin, Avila University, MO; Sydney Bassett, Auburn Global University, AL; Michael Beamer, USC, CA; Renae Betten, CBU, CA; Pepper Boyer, Auburn Global University, AL; Marina Broeder, Mission College, CA; Thomas Brynmore, Auburn Global University, AL; Britta Burton, Mission College, CA; Kathleen Castello, Mission College, CA; Teresa Cheung, North Shore Community College, MA; Shantall Colebrooke, Auburn Global University, AL; Kyle Cooper, Troy University, AL; Elizabeth Cox, Auburn Global University, AL; Ashley Ekers, Auburn Global University, AL; Rhonda Farley, Los Rios Community College, CA; Marcus Frame, Troy University, AL; Lora Glaser, Mission College, CA; Hala Hamka, Henry Ford College, MI; Shelley A. Harrington, Henry Ford College, MI; Barrett J. Heusch, Troy University, AL; Beth Hill, St. Charles Community College, MO; Patty Jones, Troy University, AL; Tom Justice, North Shore Community College, MA; Robert Klein, Troy University, AL; Patrick Maestas, Auburn Global University, AL; Elizabeth Merchant, Auburn Global University, AL; Rosemary Miketa, Henry Ford College, MI; Myo Myint, Mission College, CA; Lance Noe, Troy University, AL; Irene Pannatier, Auburn Global University, AL; Annie Percy, Troy University, AL; Erin Robinson, Troy University, AL; Juliane Rosner, Mission College, CA; Mary Stevens, North Shore Community College, MA; Pamela Stewart, Henry Ford College, MI; Karen Tucker, Georgia Tech, GA; Loreley Wheeler, North Shore Community College, MA; Amanda Wilcox, Auburn Global University, AL; Heike Williams, Auburn Global University, AL

Canada

Angelika Brunel, Collège Ahuntsic, QC; David Butler, English Language Institute, BC; Paul Edwards, Kwantlen Polytechnic University, BC; Cody Hawver, University of British Columbia, BC; Olivera Jovovic, Kwantlen Polytechnic University, BC; Tami Moffatt, University of British Columbia, BC; Dana Pynn, Vancouver Island University, BC

Latin America

Georgette Barreda, SENATI, Peru; Claudia Cecilia Díaz Romero, Colegio América, Mexico; Jeferson Ferro, Uninter, Brazil; Mayda Hernández, English Center, Mexico; Jose Ixtaccihusatl, Instituto Tecnológico de Tecomatlán, Mexico; Andreas Paulus Pabst, CBA Idiomas, Brazil; Amanda Carla Pas, Instituição de Ensino Santa Izildinha, Brazil; Allen Quesada Pacheco, University of Costa Rica, Costa Rica; Rolando Sánchez, Escuela Normal de Tecámac, Mexico; Luis Vasquez, CESNO, Mexico

Asia

Asami Atsuko, Women's University, Japan; Rene Bouchard, Chinzei Keiai Gakuen, Japan; Francis Brannen, Sangmyung University, South Korea; Haeyun Cho, Sogang University, South Korea; Daniel Craig, Sangmyung University, South Korea; Thomas Cuming, Royal Melbourne Institute of Technology, Vietnam; Jissen Joshi Daigaku, Women's University, Japan; Nguyen Duc Dat, OISP, Vietnam; Wayne Devitte, Tokai University, Japan; James D. Dunn, Tokai University, Japan; Fergus Hann, Tokai University, Japan; Michael Hood, Nihon University College of Commerce, Japan; Hideyuki Kashimoto, Shijonawate High School, Japan; David Kennedy, Nihon University, Japan; Anna Youngna Kim, Sogang University, South Korea; Jae Phil Kim, Sogang University, South Korea; Jaganathan Krishnasamy, GB Academy, Malaysia; Peter Laver, Incheon National University, South Korea; Hung Hoang Le, Ho Chi Minh City University of Technology, Vietnam; Hyon Sook Lee, Sogang University, South Korea; Ji-seon Lee, Iruda English Institute, South Korea; Joo Young Lee, Sogang University, South Korea; Phung Tu Luc, Ho Chi Minh City University of Technology, Vietnam; Richard Mansbridge, Hoa Sen University, Vietnam; Kahoko Matsumoto, Tokai University, Japan; Elizabeth May, Sangmyung University, South Korea; Naoyuki Naganuma, Tokai University, Japan; Hiroko Nishikage, Taisho University, Japan; Yongjun Park, Sangji University, South Korea; Paul Rogers, Dongguk University, South Korea; Scott Schafer, Inha University, South Korea; Michael Schvaudner, Tokai University, Japan; Brendan Smith, RMIT University, School of Languages and English, Vietnam; Peter Snashall, Huachiew Chalermprakiet University, Thailand; Makoto Takeda, Sendai Third Senior High School, Japan; Peter Talley, Mahidol University, Faculty of ICT, Thailand; Byron Thigpen, Sogang University, South Korea; Junko Yamaai, Tokai University, Japan; Junji Yamada, Taisho University, Japan; Sayoko Yamashita, Women's University, Japan; Masami Yukimori, Taisho University, Japan

Middle East and North Africa

Sajjad Ahmad, Taibah University, Saudi Arabia; Basma Alansari, Taibah University, Saudi Arabia; Marwa Al-ashqar, Taibah University, Saudi Arabia; Dr. Rashid Al-Khawaldeh, Taibah University, Saudi Arabia; Mohamed Almohamed, Taibah University, Saudi Arabia; Dr Musaad Alrahaili, Taibah University, Saudi Arabia; Hala Al Sammar, Kuwait University, Kuwait; Ahmed Alshammari, Taibah University, Saudi Arabia; Ahmed Alshamy, Taibah University, Saudi Arabia; Doniazad sultan AlShraideh, Taibah University, Saudi Arabia; Sahar Amer, Taibah University, Saudi Arabia; Nabeela Azam, Taibah University, Saudi Arabia; Hassan Bashir, Edex, Saudi Arabia; Rachel Batchilder, College of the North Atlantic, Qatar; Nicole Cuddie, Community College of Qatar, Qatar; Mahdi Duris, King Saud University, Saudi Arabia; Ahmed Ege, Institute of Public Administration, Saudi Arabia; Magda Fadle, Victoria College, Egypt; Mohammed Hassan, Taibah University, Saudi Arabia; Tom Hodgson, Community College of Qatar, Qatar; Ayub Agbar Khan, Taibah University, Saudi Arabia; Cynthia Le Joncour, Taibah University, Saudi Arabia; Ruari Alexander MacLeod, Community College of Qatar, Qatar; Nasir Mahmood, Taibah University, Saudi Arabia; Duria Salih Mahmoud, Taibah University, Saudi Arabia; Ameera McKoy, Taibah University, Saudi Arabia; Chaker Mhamdi, Buraimi University College, Oman; Baraa Shiekh Mohamed, Community College of Qatar, Qatar; Abduleelah Mohammed, Taibah University, Saudi Arabia; Shumaila Nasir, Taibah University, Saudi Arabia; Kevin Onwordi, Taibah University, Saudi Arabia; Dr. Navid Rahmani, Community College of Qatar, Qatar; Dr. Sabah Salman Sabbah, Community College of Qatar, Qatar; Salih, Taibah University, Saudi Arabia; Verna Santos-Nafrada, King Saud University, Saudi Arabia; Gamal Abdelfattah Shehata, Taibah University, Saudi Arabia; Ron Stefan, Institute of Public Administration, Saudi Arabia; Dr. Saad Torki, Imam Abdulrahman Bin Faisal University, Dammam, Saudi Arabia; Silvia Yafai, Applied Technology High School/Secondary Technical School, UAE; Mahmood Zar, Taibah University, Saudi Arabia; Thouraya Zheni, Taibah University, Saudi Arabia

Turkey

Sema Babacan, Istanbul Medipol University; Bilge Çöllüoğlu Yakar, Bilkent University; Liana Corniel, Koc University; Savas Geylanioglu, Izmir Bahcesehir Science and Technology College; Öznur Güler, Giresun University; Selen Bilginer Halefoğlu, Maltepe University; Ahmet Konukoğlu, Hasan Kalyoncu University; Mehmet Salih Yoğun, Gaziantep Hasan Kalyoncu University; Fatih Yücel, Beykent University

Europe

Irina Gerasimova, Saint-Petersburg Mining University, Russia; Amina Al Hashamia, University of Exeter, UK; Jodi, Las Dominicas, Spain; Marina Khanykova, School 179, Russia; Oksana Postnikova, Lingua Practica, Russia; Nina Vasilchenko, Soho-Bridge Language School, Russia

CRITICAL THINKING

The unique critical thinking approach of the *Q: Skills for Success* series has been further enhanced in the Third Edition. New features help you analyze, synthesize, and develop your ideas.

Unit question

The thought-provoking unit questions engage you with the topic and provide a critical thinking framework for the unit.

UNIT QUESTION

What makes a good leader?

A. Discuss these questions with your classmates.

1. Have you ever been a leader? For example, have you ever been in charge of a group at school or been the captain of a sports team? If so, what challenges did you face as a leader?

2. Think of a leader you admire. What makes this person a good leader?

Analysis

You can discuss your opinion of each listening text and analyze how it changes your perspective on the unit question.

SAY WHAT YOU THINK

SYNTHESIZE Think about Listening 1, Listening 2, and the unit video as you discuss the questions.

1. The speakers suggest that the appearance of a product or a space can send a message. What message do you send by your own appearance and the appearance of your possessions?

2. Think about a time that you judged someone based on how he or she looked or organized things. Was your first impression right or wrong? Why?

3. How can colors help a person to be more organized? How could a productive messy person use color to find things more easily?

NEW! Critical Thinking Strategy with video

Each unit includes a Critical Thinking Strategy with activities to give you step-by-step guidance in critical analysis of texts. An accompanying instructional video (available on iQ Online) provides extra support and examples.

NEW! Bloom's Taxonomy

Pink activity headings integrate verbs from Bloom's Taxonomy to help you see how each activity develops critical thinking skills.

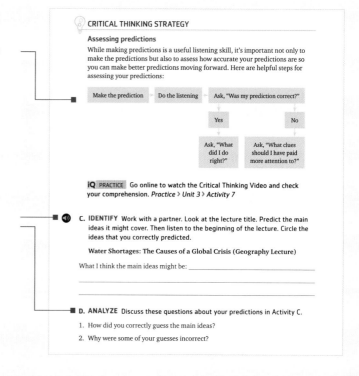

CRITICAL THINKING STRATEGY

Assessing predictions

While making predictions is a useful listening skill, it's important not only to make the predictions but also to assess how accurate your predictions are so you can make better predictions moving forward. Here are helpful steps for assessing your predictions:

Make the prediction → Do the listening → Ask, "Was my prediction correct?"

Yes → Ask, "What did I do right?"

No → Ask, "What clues should I have paid more attention to?"

iQ PRACTICE Go online to watch the Critical Thinking Video and check your comprehension. *Practice > Unit 3 > Activity 7*

C. IDENTIFY Work with a partner. Look at the lecture title. Predict the main ideas it might cover. Then listen to the beginning of the lecture. Circle the ideas that you correctly predicted.

Water Shortages: The Causes of a Global Crisis (Geography Lecture)

What I think the main ideas might be: _____

_____

_____

D. ANALYZE Discuss these questions about your predictions in Activity C.

1. How did you correctly guess the main ideas?

2. Why were some of your guesses incorrect?

THREE TYPES OF VIDEO

UNIT VIDEO

The unit videos include high-interest documentaries and reports on a wide variety of subjects, all linked to the unit topic and question.

NEW! "Work with the Video" pages guide you in watching, understanding, and discussing the unit videos. The activities help you see the connection to the Unit Question and the other texts in the unit.

NEW! In some units, one of the main listening texts is a video.

CRITICAL THINKING VIDEO

NEW! Narrated by the *Q* series authors, these short videos give you further instruction on the Critical Thinking Strategy of each unit using engaging images and graphics. You can use them to gain a deeper understanding of the Critical Thinking Strategy.

SKILLS VIDEO

NEW! These instructional videos provide illustrated explanations of skills and grammar points in the Student Book. They can be viewed in class or assigned for a flipped classroom, for homework, or for review. One skill video is available for every unit.

Easily access all videos in the Resources section of iQ Online.

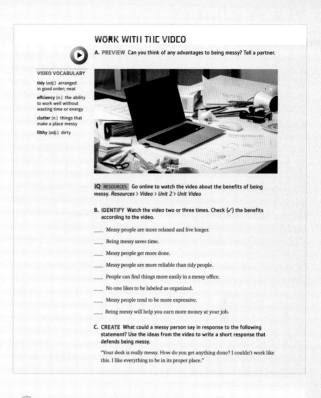

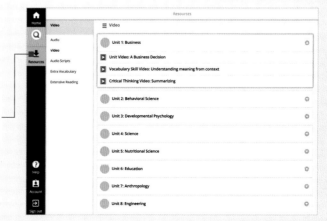

VOCABULARY

A research-based vocabulary program focuses on the words you need to know academically and professionally.

The vocabulary syllabus in *Q: Skills for Success* is correlated to the CEFR (see page 204) and linked to two word lists: the Oxford 5000 and the OPAL (Oxford Phrasal Academic Lexicon).

‌ OXFORD 5000

The Oxford 5000 is an expanded core word list for advanced learners of English. As well as the Oxford 3000 core list, the Oxford 5000 includes an additional 2,000 words, guiding learners at B2–C1 level on the most useful, high-level words to learn.

Vocabulary Key
In vocabulary activities, ‌ shows you the word is in the Oxford 5000 and **OPAL** shows you the word or phrase is in the OPAL.

PREVIEW THE LISTENING

A. PREVIEW In this lecture, the speaker presents some of the negative ways in which successful executives may change. What are two ways you think people tend to change negatively when they become leaders?

B. VOCABULARY Read aloud these words from Listening 2. Check (✓) the ones you know. Use a dictionary to define any new or unknown words. Then discuss with a partner how the words will relate to the unit.

advance *(v.)* ‌	effective *(adj.)* ‌ OPAL	style *(n.)* ‌ OPAL
assess *(v.)* ‌ OPAL	ethical *(adj.)* ‌ OPAL	title *(n.)* ‌ OPAL
capable *(adj.)* ‌ OPAL	executive *(n.)* ‌	
contact *(n.)* ‌ OPAL	perspective *(n.)* ‌ OPAL	

‌ Oxford 5000™ words   OPAL Oxford Phrasal Academic Lexicon

iQ **PRACTICE** Go online to listen and practice your pronunciation.
Practice › Unit 1 › Activity 7

OPAL
OXFORD PHRASAL ACADEMIC LEXICON

NEW! The OPAL is a collection of four word lists that provide an essential guide to the most important words and phrases to know for academic English. The word lists are based on the Oxford Corpus of Academic English and the British Academic Spoken English corpus. The OPAL includes both spoken and written academic English and both individual words and longer phrases.

Academic Language tips in the Student Book give information about how words and phrases from the OPAL are used and offer help with features such as collocations and phrases.

CATEGORIZE Read and listen to the presentation abc happy appearance. Complete the notes in the T-chart

ACADEMIC LANGUAGE
It's helpful to listen for key phrases that communicate a contrast. Phrases like *on the other hand*, *at the same time*, *rather than*, and *but in fact* tell the listener that contrasting information is coming up.

OPAL
Oxford Phrasal Academic Lexicon

Sure, we all look better when we smile, but can ou really cause us to succeed or fail? Many scientists bel lead to more success in life, while frowning can lead Some researchers discovered that people who smiled were more likely to have longer, happier marriages in those who did not. In contrast, people who didn't sm photos tended to get divorced more often. Also, peop interviews were more likely to get the jobs than cand smile. Smiling also reduces stress, some scientists say smiling while doing a stressful job helped workers' br recover from the stress more quickly afterward. On th who didn't smile had faster heartbeats long after they job. Maybe this is why smiling can even cause people research study discovered that if baseball players wei cards, they lived almost seven years longer than playe smiling. So remember to smile!

EXTENSIVE READING

Extensive Reading is a program of reading for pleasure at a level that matches your language ability.

There are many benefits to Extensive Reading:

- It helps you to become a better reader in general.
- It helps to increase your reading speed.
- It can improve your reading comprehension.
- It increases your vocabulary range.
- It can help you improve your grammar and writing skills.
- It's great for motivation to read something that is interesting for its own sake.

Each unit of *Q: Skills for Success* Third Edition has been aligned to an Oxford Graded Reader based on the appropriate topic and level of language proficiency. The first chapter of each recommended graded reader can be downloaded from iQ Online Resources.

UNIT 1

UNIT 2

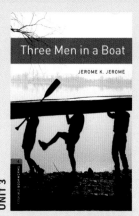

UNIT 3

UNIT 4

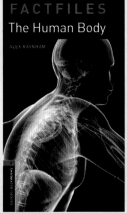

UNIT 5

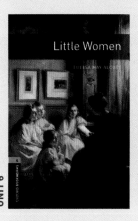

UNIT 6

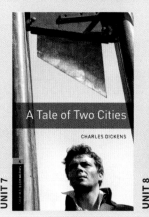

UNIT 7

UNIT 8

iQ ONLINE extends your learning beyond the classroom.

- Practice activities provide essential skills practice and support.
- Automatic grading and progress reports show you what you have mastered and where you need more practice.
- The Discussion Board allows you to discuss the Unit Questions and helps you develop your critical thinking.
- Essential resources such as audio and video are easy to access anytime.

NEW TO THE THIRD EDITION

- iQ Online is optimized for mobile use so you can use it on your phone.
- An updated interface allows easy navigation around the activities, tests, resources, and scores.
- New Critical Thinking Videos expand on the Critical Thinking Strategies in the Student Book.
- The Extensive Reading program helps you improve your vocabulary and reading skills.

How to use iQ ONLINE

Go to **Practice** to find additional practice and support to complement your learning in the classroom.

Go to **Resources** to find:
- All Student Book video
- All Student Book audio
- Critical Thinking videos
- Skills videos
- Extensive Reading

Go to **Messages** and **Discussion Board** to communicate with your teacher and classmates.

Online tests assigned by your teacher help you assess your progress and see where you need more practice.

A progress bar shows you how many activities you have completed.

View your scores for all activities.

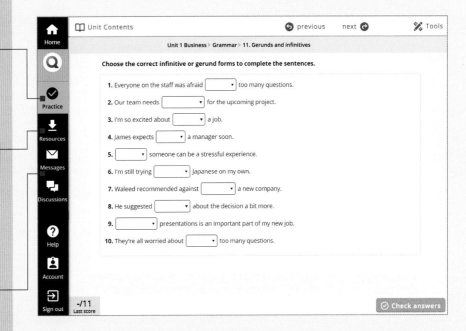

Unit Contents		previous	next	Tools

Unit 1 Business ▶ Grammar ▶ 11. Gerunds and infinitives

Choose the correct infinitive or gerund forms to complete the sentences.

1. Everyone on the staff was afraid [▼] too many questions.
2. Our team needs [▼] for the upcoming project.
3. I'm so excited about [▼] a job.
4. James expects [▼] a manager soon.
5. [▼] someone can be a stressful experience.
6. I'm still trying [▼] Japanese on my own.
7. Waleed recommended against [▼] a new company.
8. He suggested [▼] about the decision a bit more.
9. [▼] presentations is an important part of my new job.
10. They're all worried about [▼] too many questions.

-/11 Last score

✓ Check answers

My practice   🖨 Print

Q: Skills for Success Third Edition Listening and Speaking 4

Show **Last attempt** ▼   Scores **%** ▼

1	Unit 1: Business	2/21 Activities done	2%
1	Unit 1 Test	0/3 Activities done	0%

1.8

		tries	last
Unit 1 Test Activity 1		0	-
Unit 1 Test Activity 2		0	-
Unit 1 Test Activity 3		0	-

2	Unit 2: Behavioral Science	0/21 Activities done	0%
2	Unit 2 Test	0/3 Activities done	0%
3	Unit 3: Developmental Psychology	0/22	0%

ix

CONTENTS

Business

NOTE-TAKING using a chart to organize notes about main ideas
LISTENING listening for main ideas
VOCABULARY understanding meaning from context
GRAMMAR gerunds and infinitives
PRONUNCIATION syllable stress
CRITICAL THINKING summarizing
SPEAKING checking for understanding

What makes a good leader?

A. Discuss these questions with your classmates.

1. Have you ever been a leader? For example, have you ever been in charge of a group at school or been the captain of a sports team? If so, what challenges did you face as a leader?

2. Think of a leader you admire. What makes this person a good leader?

3. Look at the photo. Identify the leader. What qualities might make this person an effective leader?

B. Listen to *The Q Classroom* online. Then answer these questions.

1. Yuna feels that leaders should act more responsibly when they have power. Do you agree? Why or why not?

2. Felix says that becoming a leader makes a person's life difficult in some ways. Do you agree? If so, in what ways do you think becoming a leader would make a person's life difficult?

iQ PRACTICE Go to the online discussion board to discuss the Unit Question with your classmates. *Practice > Unit 1 > Activity 1*

UNIT OBJECTIVE

Listen to a radio interview and a lecture and gather information and ideas to give a presentation about how to be an effective leader.

NOTE-TAKING SKILL Using a chart to organize notes about main ideas

Charts are a useful way to organize your notes on a presentation. Using a chart to list main ideas can help you understand how a presentation is organized and can help you identify the speaker's most important points.

To organize your notes about main ideas, divide your page into two columns. Use the left column to show how the presentation is organized. Use the right column to write down the main ideas. You can also write any key words or phrases that support each main idea.

Look at the example below from Activity A. The student uses the left column to show the topics in a text and the right column to show the main ideas and key phrases.

Topic: Motivating teams	Main ideas and key phrases
First way	Make expectations clear
	- gives team a goal

A. IDENTIFY Listen to part of a talk about motivating team members. Note the main ideas in the chart.

Topic: Motivating teams	Main ideas and key phrases
First way	Make expectations clear — gives team a goal —
Second way	
Third way	

B. APPLY Listen again. In the chart, add key words and phrases that support each main idea. Compare your notes with a partner. Then take turns coming up with your own examples of each way to motivate team members.

iQ PRACTICE Go online for more practice using a chart to organize notes about main ideas. *Practice > Unit 1 > Activity 2*

LISTENING 1

OBJECTIVE ▶

Leadership Isn't Just for the Boss

You are going to listen to a radio interview from the Canadian Broadcasting Company about leadership at all levels of an organization. As you listen to the conversation, gather information and ideas about leadership qualities and how organizations can create leadership opportunities across their workforce.

PREVIEW THE LISTENING

A. PREVIEW Before you listen, discuss the questions in a small group.

1. What are some important leadership qualities? What adjectives describe good leaders?

2. Former American president John Quincy Adams said, "If your actions inspire others to dream more, learn more, do more, and become more, you are a leader." What do you think this quote means? Do you agree?

B. VOCABULARY Read aloud these words from Listening 1. Check (✓) the ones you know. Use a dictionary to define any new or unknown words. Then discuss with a partner how the words will relate to the unit.

clarity *(n.)* 🔑	**motivation** *(n.)* 🔑 OPAL	**role** *(n.)* 🔑 OPAL
enthusiasm *(n.)* 🔑	**promote** *(v.)* 🔑 OPAL	**take on** *(v. phr.)* 🔑
initiative *(n.)* 🔑 OPAL	**realistic** *(adj.)* 🔑	**versus** *(prep.)* 🔑 OPAL
innovation *(n.)* 🔑	**responsibility** *(n.)* 🔑 OPAL	

🔑 Oxford 5000™ words   OPAL Oxford Phrasal Academic Lexicon

iQ PRACTICE Go online to listen and practice your pronunciation.
Practice > Unit 1 > Activity 3

WORK WITH THE LISTENING

 A. LISTEN AND TAKE NOTES Listen to the radio interview and take notes on the speaker's central ideas and suggestions. Write the main ideas and key phrases you hear.

iQ RESOURCES Go online to download extra vocabulary support.
Resources > Extra Vocabulary > Unit 1

Leadership topics	Main ideas and key phrases
Important leadership qualities	
What organizations can do to encourage leadership at all levels	
Benefits to having leadership at all levels	

B. CATEGORIZE Read the statements. Write *T* (true) or *F* (false). Then correct each false statement to make it true.

_____ 1. Effective companies put all their workers in leadership roles.

_____ 2. One way companies can encourage leadership is by creating opportunities for people to work with other teams.

_____ 3. A lack of clarity in organizations creates opportunities for creativity.

_____ 4. Demonstrating initiative is a good way to be leader-like.

_____ 5. Good leaders build relationships by leaving employees alone.

 C. IDENTIFY Read the sentences. Then listen again. Circle the correct answers.

1. Why is it good for a company to create opportunities for people to act more leader-like at all levels?

   a. Because having a lot of supervisors means more work gets done

   b. Because doing so promotes innovation, creativity, and motivation

   c. Because more responsibility makes workers happier

2. What is the benefit to having employees work outside their teams?

    a. They can form more friendships at work.

    b. They can share the work and get finished faster.

    c. They have an opportunity to try different things.

3. What do organizations have to have in order for their employees to thrive?

    a. Clear expectations and goals

    b. Enough room to have many leadership positions

    c. A fun work environment

4. How can people demonstrate initiative at work?

    a. By taking on a task without waiting for direction

    b. By telling their boss what he or she is doing wrong

    c. By coming early in the morning

5. Why should workers try to be friendly at work?

    a. Because it will make them feel happier

    b. Because their boss will want to spend time with them

    c. Because their attitude will motivate their co-workers

D. INTERPRET Read the comments below. Based on the listening, are the speakers demonstrating leader-like qualities? Write _Y_ (yes) or _N_ (no).

____ 1. "When I get to work, I get right to business. After all, the company isn't paying me to chat with my co-workers."

____ 2. "I am a low-level manager in a big company. I expect my employees to obey me because I am their boss. They don't need to know why I tell them to do things."

____ 3. "I enjoy working on projects with other departments. It sparks my creativity when I think outside the box."

____ 4. "I don't like to take on too much responsibility at work. It's important to me to have free time for my real interests and hobbies. Work is just a way to make money for life."

____ 5. "I think it's important for my employees to understand my plan for the company and for them to be clear about the direction I want the company to go in."

____ 6. "Even when I am not feeling it, I try to demonstrate my excitement to be at work. I want my employees to know that I am excited about our company. I hope they feel motivated, too."

E. CREATE Work with a partner. If you were the head of an organization, how would you make sure to hire people who demonstrated leadership qualities? Create questions that you could ask potential employees in a job interview to determine whether they are leader-like.

F. VOCABULARY Here are some words from Listening 1. Complete each sentence with the correct word.

clarity *(n.)*	innovation *(n.)*	realistic *(adj.)*	take on *(v. phr.)*
enthusiasm *(n.)*	motivation *(n.)*	responsibility *(n.)*	versus *(prep.)*
initiative *(n.)*	promote *(v.)*	role *(n.)*	

1. Young people are often responsible for much of the exciting _____ happening in the tech world because they often have new and fresh ideas.

2. An employee's _____ is the part that person plays in the organization.

3. Some animals _____ the colors of their environments so they can hide from predators better.

4. Many people say that money is the main _____ for working.

5. The company bought time on a TV station to _____ its new product.

6. It's not _____ to think you will ever win the lottery.

7. If you want to get ahead at work, you need to show some _____ by taking on responsibilities without being asked first.

8. Looking the word up in the dictionary gave me a lot of _____. I really feel like I understand the text better now.

9. When you are choosing a career, you need to compare the benefits of money _____ job satisfaction.

10. She does her job with such _____ that it's fun to work with her.

11. Good supervisors take _____ for their employees.

iQ PRACTICE Go online for more practice with the vocabulary.
Practice > Unit 1 > Activity 4

iQ PRACTICE Go online for additional listening and comprehension.
Practice > Unit 1 > Activity 5

SAY WHAT YOU THINK

DISCUSS Work in a group to discuss the questions.

1. The interview discussed the benefits of encouraging leader-like behavior at all levels. What are some possible disadvantages?

2. Recall the leadership qualities the speaker described in the radio interview. Share examples of times you have shown these qualities.

LISTENING SKILL Listening for main ideas

When listening to a presentation, it is difficult to remember every piece of information you hear. Instead of trying to remember every detail, it is more important to identify the speaker's **main ideas**. These are the most important ideas that the speaker wants you to understand and remember.

A speaker often states the main ideas as part of the introduction. Here are some signal phrases used to introduce main ideas.

> Today <u>we'll focus on</u> . . .
>
> This morning <u>we'll consider</u> . . .
>
> Today <u>I'm going to talk about</u> . . .
>
> For today's lecture, <u>we're going to look at</u> . . .

Main ideas are often repeated or rephrased during a presentation, especially at the end.

After you listen and take notes, review your notes. Notice which ideas are repeated or described in greater detail. This will help you decide what the main ideas are.

 A. EVALUATE Listen to the introduction to each of three presentations. Circle the option that best describes the main idea of each introduction.

ACADEMIC LANGUAGE

In academic writing, the main ideas are often presented indirectly. However, speakers usually directly introduce their main ideas by using the future tense in phrases like *I'm going to show you . . .*, *we're going to go through . . .*, and *we're going to be talking about . . .*

_____ OPAL
Oxford Phrasal Academic Lexicon

Introduction 1:

a. Meetings are often boring because they're too long and waste time.

b. Meetings are often boring, but there are ways to make them worthwhile.

c. Meetings are often boring, so we should find ways to eliminate them.

Introduction 2:

a. Job searchers should learn how to answer interview questions and write résumés.

b. Job searchers should learn how to use online job-finding tools effectively.

c. Job searchers should go online to find out about available jobs.

Introduction 3:

    a. Many people hire employees for the wrong reasons. Soon they regret their hiring decisions.

    b. It is important that managers learn to recognize that someone is not a good hiring choice.

    c. Hiring employees can be difficult, but this presentation will teach skills for choosing the best possible employees.

B. APPLY Listen to a short presentation. As you listen, take notes in the chart.

Topic	
Most important factor	
First characteristic mentioned	
Second characteristic mentioned	
Last characteristic mentioned	

iQ PRACTICE Go online for more practice listening for main ideas.
Practice > Unit 1 > Activity 6

Myths of Effective Leadership

You are going to listen to a lecture from the Center for Creative Leadership, an organization dedicated to helping executives by providing them with the information and skills they need to lead well and overcome common challenges. As you listen to the lecture, gather information and ideas about what makes a good leader.

PREVIEW THE LISTENING

A. PREVIEW In this lecture, the speaker presents some of the negative ways in which successful executives may change. What are two ways you think people tend to change negatively when they become leaders?

B. VOCABULARY Read aloud these words from Listening 2. Check (✓) the ones you know. Use a dictionary to define any new or unknown words. Then discuss with a partner how the words will relate to the unit.

advance *(v.)* 🔒	**effective** *(adj.)* 🔒 OPAL	**style** *(n.)* 🔒 OPAL
assess *(v.)* 🔒 OPAL	**ethical** *(adj.)* 🔒 OPAL	**title** *(n.)* 🔒 OPAL
capable *(adj.)* 🔒 OPAL	**executive** *(n.)* 🔒	
contact *(n.)* 🔒 OPAL	**perspective** *(n.)* 🔒 OPAL	

🔒 Oxford 5000™ words   OPAL Oxford Phrasal Academic Lexicon

iQ PRACTICE Go online to listen and practice your pronunciation.
Practice > Unit 1 > Activity 7

WORK WITH THE LISTENING

 A. LISTEN AND TAKE NOTES Listen to the lecture and take notes in the charts.

iQ RESOURCES   Go online to download extra vocabulary support.
Resources > Extra Vocabulary > Unit 1

Actions of ineffective leaders	Main ideas and key phrases
First example	
Second example	
Third example	

Advice for leaders	Main ideas and key phrases
First piece of advice	
Second piece of advice	
Third piece of advice	

B. EXPLAIN Use your notes to answer the questions.

1. According to a study by the Center for Creative Leadership, how do many powerful executives see themselves?

2. What do many powerful executives think about people who disagree with them?

3. How do these employees begin to react to the executives?

C. CATEGORIZE Read the statements. Then listen again. Write *T* (true) or *F* (false). Then correct each false statement to make it true.

____ 1. Many executives forget the skills that helped them become successful.

____ 2. An effective executive must know the difference between power and leadership.

____ 3. A study shows that many executives respect employees who disagree with them.

____ 4. Many executives begin to believe they are more powerful than they really are.

____ 5. It is impossible to learn the skills necessary for effective leadership.

____ 6. To become an effective leader, you must view yourself through the eyes of your team members.

D. EVALUATE Read the advice on leadership. Check (✓) the advice you think the speaker would agree with. Briefly discuss your ideas with a partner.

☐ 1. When team members disagree with you, ask some questions and take time to consider their perspectives.

☐ 2. Encourage your team members to ask questions about your decisions and plans.

☐ 3. Instead of personal meetings, announce major business decisions and plans by email or video.

☐ 4. Invite team members to fill out anonymous feedback forms about your performance and your leadership style.

☐ 5. Keep your contact with team members brief. If they have concerns or complaints, encourage them to speak with your assistant.

E. CATEGORIZE Read the examples of decisions made by leaders. Based on the information in the lecture, do they demonstrate effective or ineffective leadership? Write *E* (effective) or *I* (ineffective). Then discuss your choices with a partner.

_____ 1. The president of Linear Electronics, James Yoo, hires all managers from outside his company. He doesn't believe in promoting existing team members to management positions.

_____ 2. Reggie Silva, head coach of the Tower University baseball team, has breakfast with players individually each month to find out how they are doing.

_____ 3. Restaurant owner Claudia Tavares placed an "idea box" near the door of her restaurant. She checks it each week for thoughts from her customers.

_____ 4. Daniel Lisa was elected president of his university's engineering club. He assigned people who voted for him to all the advisory board positions.

_____ 5. Edgar Molina, vice president of Trident Bank, tries to read several leadership books each year.

_____ 6. Governor Patricia Landon keeps her office door open so team members can come in and talk whenever they want to.

_____ 7. The head of the English Literature Department, Coleen Zhang, believes it is much more efficient to make most departmental decisions on her own. Involving others in the decision-making process takes too long.

F. DISCUSS Work in a group to discuss the questions.

1. The speaker states that leadership and power are not the same. What do you think are some differences between leadership and power?

2. According to the lecture, some successful executives begin to "blur the lines" between leadership and power. They act as if leadership and power are the same thing. Why do you think this happens?

G. VOCABULARY Here are some words from Listening 2. Complete each sentence with the correct word.

advance *(v.)*	contact *(n.)*	executive *(n.)*	title *(n.)*
assess *(v.)*	effective *(adj.)*	perspective *(n.)*	
capable *(adj.)*	ethical *(adj.)*	style *(n.)*	

1. We need to hire a more _____ office assistant. The current assistant doesn't have enough experience and isn't highly skilled.

2. My management _____ is very different from Roger's. I prefer to lead by example. He prefers to give detailed instructions to employees.

3. I'm nervous about the meeting with my manager next Monday. She is going to _____ my performance for this year.

4. Blake joined the company in 2000. Within five years he was able to _____ to the position of vice president.

5. Please tell me what you think about this design. I'm interested in hearing your _____ on it.

6. Anne knows a lot of people in our industry. She has a good business _____ at the London office who can help us.

7. I am concerned that our company is not making _____ decisions. Our factory creates more pollution and waste than it needs to.

8. We created a plan to save the company. Unfortunately, it was not as _____ as we had hoped, and the company was forced to close last month.

9. I called her *Mrs. Rodgers*, but later I learned that her _____ is actually *Doctor*.

10. Emma only recently started working for the company, but her goal is to become a(n) _____ there someday. I think she will make a good manager.

iQ PRACTICE Go online for more practice with the vocabulary.
Practice > Unit 1 > Activity 8

WORK WITH THE VIDEO

A. PREVIEW Have you had to make any difficult decisions that affected many people? What happened?

VIDEO VOCABULARY

CEO (*n.*) chief executive officer; the person with the highest rank in a business company

gut-check moment (*idm.*) a test of one's courage, character, or determination

decline (*n.*) a continuous decrease in number, value, quality, etc., of something

viral (*adj.*) used to describe a piece of information, a video, an image, etc., that is sent rapidly over the Internet from one person to another

John Donahoe

iQ RESOURCES Go online to watch the video about a business leader who had to make some difficult decisions. *Resources* ❯ *Video* ❯ *Unit 1* ❯ *Unit Video*

B. CATEGORIZE Watch the video two or three times. Number the following events in chronological order.

_____ Employees, sellers, investors, and the media became upset.

_____ John Donahoe was appointed as the CEO of eBay.

_____ John Donahoe faced the sellers at the eBay Live meeting in Chicago and clearly explained why it was the right decision.

_____ John Donahoe reconsidered his decision overnight.

_____ John Donahoe announced his plan for big changes to eBay.

_____ John Donahoe felt personally attacked when watching online videos.

_____ Sellers started to organize to try to get rid of John Donahoe.

C. DISCUSS What lessons do you think John Donahoe learned from this experience? Share your opinions with a partner.

SAY WHAT YOU THINK

SYNTHESIZE Think about Listening 1, Listening 2, and the unit video as you discuss the questions.

1. Think of a leader you have met in your work or school life. Was he or she more like the leader in Listening 1 or Listening 2? Explain.

2. Listening 1, Listening 2, and the unit video all offer advice to bosses. Which advice do you think is the most valuable? Do you disagree with any of it? Why?

One way to figure out the meaning of a word is from the **context** of the sentence it is in. Use the words around the unknown word to help you understand the new word.

> And that night, I <u>tossed and turned</u>, and the next morning, I said, you know what, it's worth it.

The speaker talks about "night" and "the next morning," so you can understand that "tossing and turning" is something a person might do at night.

It also helps to consider the conversation as a whole, not just one sentence. In this conversation, the speaker is talking about a big decision he had to make that he was really stressed about. From this context, you might be able to figure out that *toss and turn* means to stay awake and think about something.

iQ RESOURCES Go online to watch the Vocabulary Skill Video.
Resources > Video > Unit 1 > Vocabulary Skill Video

A. APPLY Listen to the sentences below. Use the context to match each bold word with its definition in the box.

a. natural ability to do something
b. the conditions that affect a person's behavior and development
c. to work in the correct way
d. to find an acceptable solution to a problem
e. to show or display

_____ 1. The job didn't pay very well, but I loved the office and my co-workers. It was a great **environment** to work in.

_____ 2. It's impossible to **function** well when you don't get along with your co-workers. I can't work in a situation like that.

_____ 3. I'm sure you can **resolve** the conflict with your co-worker if you listen to each other's opinions.

_____ 4. James has great **aptitude**, but he needs more training. In a year or so, he'll probably be our best programmer.

_____ 5. The members of Emily's group are experienced and talented. Besides, they **exhibit** great teamwork.

B. IDENTIFY Listen to excerpts from Listening 1 and Listening 2. Circle the correct answers.

1. **Distinction** probably means ____.

   a. similarity

   b. importance

   c. difference

2. **Comfort zone** probably means ____.

   a. a new or different situation

   b. a situation in which you feel secure

   c. a situation that is dangerous

3. **Be tasked with** probably means ____.

   a. be given a job

   b. be asked a question

   c. have fun at work

4. **Opposing** probably means ____.

   a. smart

   b. contrasting

   c. similar

5. **Perceive** probably means ____.

   a. view

   b. enjoy

   c. dislike

C. CREATE Choose five words from Activities A and B. Write a sentence using each word. Then take turns reading your sentences aloud to a partner.

iQ PRACTICE Go online for more practice understanding meaning from context. *Practice > Unit 1 > Activity 9*

SPEAKING

OBJECTIVE ▶   At the end of this unit, you are going to give a presentation about how to be an effective leader. As you give the presentation, you will need to check that your audience understands you.

GRAMMAR Gerunds and infinitives

Gerunds (verb + –*ing*) are often used as the subject of a sentence.

☐ **Leading** your team members is a tough job.

Gerunds are also used after prepositions, such as *about, of, in, for*, and *against*, and after certain verbs, such as *consider, suggest*, and *recommend*.

☐ Joe thought **about accepting** the promotion.
☐ I **considered voting** for him.

Infinitives (*to* + verb) are often used after the adjective phrase *be* + adjective.

☐ It **is important to respect** your employees.

Infinitives are also used after certain verbs, such as *want, decide, try, hope, need, expect, agree*, and *learn*.

☐ She **hopes to become** a manager one day.

A. IDENTIFY Read the sentences. Underline each gerund and infinitive.

1. While every company needs a great leader, some of the most effective ones encourage their workers to take on some kind of leadership role as well.

2. What's helpful is to have leadership qualities at every level.

3. There actually is a distinction between being in a leadership role versus being a leader in your role.

4. Individuals would take initiative without waiting to get direction.

5. It gives them the opportunity to try something new.

6. So being really clear on the roles and expectations is a big thing that you can do.

7. We pay you to come to work to do your job.

8. Running a company can be a lonely, stressful experience.

9. What do you need to start a business and be successful?

10. Good leaders make people excited about being in the workplace.

B. APPLY Complete each sentence with the gerund or infinitive form of the verb in parentheses. Then practice saying the sentences with a partner.

1. Haya expects _____ (finish) business school in June.

2. This book recommends _____ (hire) people you already know.

3. _____ (work) for the government has been a great learning experience.

4. It is difficult _____ (work) while you go to school.

5. Although it took me several months, I finally learned _____ (communicate) effectively with my manager.

6. I suggest _____ (discuss) this with your partner before you make a final decision.

7. We need _____ (discuss) this problem immediately.

8. Jamal was interested in _____ (move) to Hong Kong, but he decided _____ (wait) until next year.

iQ PRACTICE Go online for more practice with gerunds and infinitives.
Practice > Unit 1 > Activities 10–11

Every word with more than one **syllable** has a syllable that is **stressed** more than the others. That stressed syllable is longer, and it has a change in pitch.

Listen to the word *negotiate*. Then repeat it.

☐ negotiate

The second syllable (*-go-*) is stressed. The vowel in this syllable is extra long, and it has a change in pitch.

Listen to the word again and practice saying it, stressing the second syllable.

☐ negotiate

Every word has its own stress pattern. Using correct word stress will make your speech clearer and easier to understand. When you learn a new word, also take note of the correct stress pattern for that word.

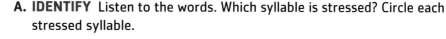

A. IDENTIFY Listen to the words. Which syllable is stressed? Circle each stressed syllable.

TIP FOR SUCCESS

Many dictionaries show a pronunciation guide for each entry. The pronunciation guide shows the correct syllable stress. Use a dictionary regularly to learn the stress patterns of new words.

1. excerpt
2. aspect
3. enforce
4. effective

5. leadership
6. acknowledge
7. perspective
8. opposing

9. promotion
10. interaction

B. APPLY Listen again. Then practice with a partner. Take turns saying the words.

iQ PRACTICE Go online for more practice with syllable stress.
Practice > Unit 1 > Activity 12

CRITICAL THINKING STRATEGY

Summarizing

When you **summarize**, you give a shorter version of what you heard or read, including only the main points. You should not include minor details, direct quotes, or your own opinion. Summarizing shows you understand the material.

iQ PRACTICE Go online to watch the Critical Thinking Video and check your comprehension. *Practice > Unit 1 > Activity 13*

C. COMPOSE Listen to the presentation and take notes. Work with a partner to summarize the main points.

D. DISCUSS Work in a small group. Compare your summaries and choose the most complete summary.

When you're giving a presentation or having a conversation, occasionally check that you are clearly communicating your ideas. To check that your listeners understand your main point(s), you can use phrases like these.

Do you know what I mean?	Are you following me?
Does that make sense?	Any questions (so far)?
Do you understand?	

A. IDENTIFY Listen to a manager giving instructions to his staff. Check (✓) the phrases he uses to check for understanding.

☐ Do you know what I mean?   ☐ Are you following me?

☐ Do you know what I'm saying?   ☐ Are you with me so far?

☐ Does that make sense?   ☐ Have you got it?

☐ Does everyone understand?   ☐ Got it?

B. RESTATE Listen again. Then work with a partner. Summarize the main points the manager wants to communicate.

iQ PRACTICE Go online for more practice checking for understanding. *Practice > Unit 1 > Activity 14*

UNIT ASSIGNMENT Give a presentation on how to be an effective leader

OBJECTIVE ▶

In this assignment, you are going to give a short presentation about how to be an effective leader. As you prepare your presentation, think about the Unit Question, "What makes a good leader?" Use information from Listening 1, Listening 2, the unit video, and your work in this unit to support your presentation. Refer to the Self-Assessment checklist on page 24.

CONSIDER THE IDEAS

DISCUSS Read about a paradox, a situation that has two opposite qualities at the same time. In a group, discuss what the author means by a *power paradox*.

The Power Paradox

The best leaders understand the needs and goals of the people they lead. They are careful thinkers who understand the challenges they face. They have the ability to make intelligent choices about how to address those challenges. Great leaders are also communicators. They can explain both problems and solutions to people in a way that everyone can understand.

These abilities are not common, and when we recognize them in someone—in the business world or some other field—we are inspired to say, "That's someone I can trust! That's someone I can follow!" Unfortunately, these abilities also tend to disappear once a person actually takes on a position of leadership.

The British historian Lord Acton once said, "Power tends to corrupt, and absolute power corrupts absolutely." Researchers are now finding scientific support for Acton's claim. Many studies have shown that power can lead people to act without thinking carefully about their decisions. It can also lead people to ignore or misunderstand other people's feelings and desires.

Researchers have created experiments to see how people react when they are given power. The people who were given power over others were more likely to make risky choices, to act aggressively, to speak rudely, and to behave in ways that made others feel scared and uncomfortable. They were also more likely to tease their colleagues.

This is why we call it the *power paradox*. Power is given to people who show an ability to understand, guide, and communicate with others. But, unfortunately, once they become leaders, their power has the potential to make them rude and insensitive. In other words, what people respect and want most from leaders is often what can be damaged when someone has power.

PREPARE AND SPEAK

A. GATHER IDEAS Review the information in "The Power Paradox" about how power can affect people. Then think about the information you learned in this unit about people in positions of power. Discuss these questions with a partner.

1. What are some important skills and qualities of a leader?

2. What are negative effects that come from having power?

B. ORGANIZE IDEAS Choose two qualities and two problems from Activity A that you think are most important. Place these ideas in the first column of a chart. In a second column, list ways to develop those qualities and ways to avoid the negative effects.

C. SPEAK Present your advice to the class. As you speak, check that your classmates understand the ideas you are trying to communicate. Refer to the Self-Assessment checklist below before you begin.

iQ PRACTICE Go online for your alternate Unit Assignment.
Practice › Unit 1 › Activity 15

CHECK AND REFLECT

A. CHECK Think about the Unit Assignment as you complete the Self-Assessment checklist.

SELF-ASSESSMENT	Yes	No
I was able to speak easily about the topic.	☐	☐
My partner, group, and class understood me.	☐	☐
I understood meaning from context.	☐	☐
I used vocabulary from the unit.	☐	☐
I checked for understanding.	☐	☐
I used correct syllable stress.	☐	☐

B. REFLECT Discuss these questions with a partner or group.

1. What is something new you learned in this unit?

2. Look back at the Unit Question—What makes a good leader? Is your answer different now than when you started this unit? If yes, how is it different? Why?

iQ PRACTICE Go to the online discussion board to discuss the questions.
Practice › Unit 1 › Activity 16

TRACK YOUR SUCCESS

iQ PRACTICE Go online to check the words and phrases you have learned in this unit. *Practice > Unit 1 > Activity 17*

Check (✓) the skills and strategies you learned. If you need more work on a skill, refer to the page(s) in parentheses.

NOTE-TAKING	☐ I can use a chart to organize notes about main ideas. (p. 4)
LISTENING	☐ I can listen for main ideas. (p. 9)
VOCABULARY	☐ I can understand meaning from context. (p. 17)
GRAMMAR	☐ I can use gerunds and infinitives. (p. 19)
PRONUNCIATION	☐ I can use syllable stress. (p. 21)
CRITICAL THINKING	☐ I can summarize information. (p. 21)
SPEAKING	☐ I can check for understanding. (p. 22)

OBJECTIVE ▶ ☐ I can gather information and ideas to give a presentation on how to be an effective leader.

Behavioral Science

How does appearance affect our success?

A. Discuss these questions with your classmates.

1. Think about a product you recently bought. How did the appearance (color, shape, size) affect your decision to buy it?

2. Do you think people who are organized are also more likely to be successful? How might appearing organized make someone seem successful?

3. Look at the photo. What does this workspace tell you about the people who work here? Would you like to work in a space like this? Why or why not?

B. Listen to *The Q Classroom* online. Then answer these questions.

1. Sophy believes that how we dress affects what people think of us. Do you agree or disagree? Why?

2. Felix argues that not all successful people need to dress well. In addition to athletes, what professionals might have more freedom when it comes to deciding what to wear?

iQ PRACTICE Go to the online discussion board to discuss the Unit Question with your classmates. *Practice > Unit 2 > Activity 1*

UNIT OBJECTIVE

Listen to a book review and a podcast and gather information and ideas to role-play a conversation offering advice to help someone become better organized.

LISTENING

LISTENING 1   A Perfect Mess

OBJECTIVE ▶

You are going to listen to a review of a book about mess. The book compares people who are neat to people who aren't. It explores who is more successful. As you listen to the review, gather information and ideas about how appearance affects our success.

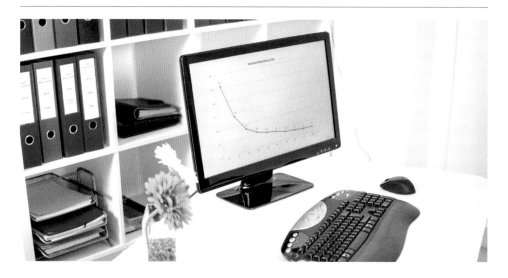

PREVIEW THE LISTENING

A. PREVIEW Look at the statements below. Check (✓) the statements you agree with.

☐ Messy people are never very organized.

☐ Children should not focus too much on neatness.

☐ Neatness is required in order to work effectively.

☐ It is OK to be a little messy at home.

B. VOCABULARY Read aloud these words from Listening 1. Check (✓) the ones you know. Use a dictionary to define any new or unknown words. Then discuss with a partner how the words will relate to the unit.

bias *(n.)* ℞ OPAL	moderately *(adv.)*	stifle *(v.)*
chaos *(n.)* ℞	open-minded *(adj.)*	stimulating *(adj.)*
embrace *(v.)* ℞	point out *(v. phr.)* ℞	stumble upon *(v. phr.)*
inflexible *(adj.)*	recognize *(v.)* ℞ OPAL	turn out *(v. phr.)* ℞

℞ Oxford 5000™ words   OPAL Oxford Phrasal Academic Lexicon

iQ PRACTICE Go online to listen and practice your pronunciation.
Practice > Unit 2 > Activity 2

WORK WITH THE LISTENING

A. LISTEN AND TAKE NOTES Listen to the review and take notes in the chart.

iQ RESOURCES Go online to download extra vocabulary support.
Resources > Extra Vocabulary > Unit 2

Benefits of being messy	Main ideas and key phrases
At work	
At home	

B. EXPLAIN Imagine you were the police chief in Pennsylvania who was fired because of his messy desk. Use your notes to explain why you should get your job back. Write two or three sentences and share them with a partner.

C. CATEGORIZE Read the statements. Write *T* (true) or *F* (false). Then correct each false statement to make it true.

____ 1. Moderate messiness seems to be good for people.

____ 2. Messy homes are cold and impersonal.

____ 3. Messy environments are not stimulating enough for children.

____ 4. Messy people tend to be more creative and open-minded.

D. IDENTIFY Read the sentences. Then listen again. Circle the answer that best completes each statement.

1. ____ was a very messy but open-minded author.

   a. Albert Einstein

   b. Leon Heppel

   c. Agatha Christie

2. Keeping a house too ____ can be bad for a child's health.

   a. clean

   b. dirty

   c. stimulating

3. A messy desk helped ____ two researchers' work.

   a. cause confusion about

   b. show a connection between

   c. find errors in

4. No one interviewed at the NAPO conference could answer the question ____.

   a. "Why are people fined at work?"

   b. "What's wrong with being messy?"

   c. "Why is there a bias toward neatness?"

5. Henry Rubins liked his room to be messy because ____.

   a. chaos made him feel comfortable

   b. he had to be neat at work

   c. it made his mother angry

6. A woman in Australia was fined more than $2,000 because she had ____.

   a. too many personal items on her desk

   b. a lot of papers all over her desk

   c. a messy desk

Leon Heppel

E. CATEGORIZE Read the sentences about the two examples of messy success stories. Who is each sentence about? Write *LH* (Leon Heppel) or *AC* (Agatha Christie).

____ 1. This messy person was a researcher at the National Institutes of Health.

____ 2. This messy person compared the information in two different letters.

____ 3. This messy person wrote ideas in disorganized notebooks.

____ 4. This messy person won a Nobel Prize.

____ 5. This messy person wrote very popular novels.

____ 6. This messy person lost important notebooks in the mess on the desk.

F. VOCABULARY Here are some words from Listening 1. Read the sentences. Circle the answer that best matches the meaning of each bold word or phrase.

1. We hope everyone will **embrace** our new plan for the class trip. We think you will really like the new destination!

   a. be unwilling to accept

   b. accept an idea with enthusiasm

   c. be concerned about

Agatha Christie

VOCABULARY SKILL REVIEW

In Unit 1, you learned about understanding meaning from context. Remember to search the context of an unknown word for clues about its meaning. Look beyond the word's phrase to the sentence or even the text as a whole.

2. I don't want to **stifle** your creativity, but your ideas for the brochure are too complicated. Let's try to make it very simple.

   a. let go of something

   b. prevent something from happening

   c. support something strongly

3. Parents often have a **bias** toward their own children and think they are better than other children.

   a. hope for

   b. a thought about

   c. preference for

4. You need to **point out** in your job application why you think you are qualified for the job. It's important that the interviewer understand your skills and experience.

   a. look at something carefully

   b. make something clear

   c. consider someone's ideas

5. The student was **moderately** successful last semester. He didn't fail any classes, but he didn't get excellent grades, either.

   a. not at all

   b. fairly, but not very

   c. extremely

6. I couldn't find my book, and then I happened to **stumble upon** it at my friend's house. It was there the whole time!

   a. find by accident

   b. hit quickly

   c. damage

7. We worked hard all week, but finally we had to **recognize** that we weren't going to finish the project on time.

   a. acknowledge

   b. discourage

   c. ignore

8. The museum was **stimulating**. I was so excited about what I saw that I went back the next day.

   a. expensive

   b. boring

   c. interesting

9. I was worried, but I think the event will **turn out** fine. It looks like we have everything under control.

    a. increase to a new level

    b. change direction quickly

    c. happen with a particular result

10. I am an **open-minded** person. Just because something is different doesn't mean I won't like it.

    a. afraid of trying new things

    b. careless with someone's property

    c. willing to accept new ideas or opinions

11. The chef is very **inflexible**. He always uses the same recipes. He does not like to try new ideas.

    a. unfriendly to others

    b. unsure of the answer

    c. unwilling to change

12. The little boy's room was complete **chaos**. Books, clothes, and games were scattered all over the floor.

    a. a big mess

    b. orderly and neat

    c. well organized

iQ PRACTICE Go online for more practice with the vocabulary.
Practice > Unit 2 > Activity 3

iQ PRACTICE Go online for additional listening and comprehension.
Practice > Unit 2 > Activity 4

? SAY WHAT YOU THINK

DISCUSS Work in a group to discuss the questions.

1. How messy are you? Do you agree with the authors of *A Perfect Mess* about the benefits of being a bit messy? Why or why not?

2. How much freedom to be messy should workers have in their workspace?

3. When you were a child, were you neat or messy? Have you changed at all as you have gotten older? How?

LISTENING SKILL Identifying details

When you listen to a long presentation or lecture, it's difficult to take notes on everything. It's important to focus on details that support the main ideas you hear.

Ask yourself three questions as you listen.

- Is this new information?
- Does this information support the main idea?
- Is this information repeated or rephrased?

If you answer *yes* to any of these questions, the detail may be important to remember.

A. CATEGORIZE Listen to a short lecture about three strategies for being more organized. Complete the chart with important details about each strategy.

TIP FOR SUCCESS

Use abbreviations and symbols when you take notes. This will make it easier to take notes quickly. Then review your notes to make sure your ideas are clear.

Strategy	Main ideas and key phrases

B. EVALUATE Work with a partner. Compare your notes. Ask each other the following questions. If you answer *no* to a question, revise your notes.

1. Does this information support the main idea?

2. Is this information repeated or rephrased?

iQ PRACTICE Go online for more practice identifying details.
Practice > Unit 2 > Activity 5

NOTE-TAKING SKILL Taking notes to compare and contrast

A T-chart is useful for taking notes about two contrasting topics. When you are reading a text or listening to something about two sides of an issue or two different ideas, make a T-chart by drawing a "T." Write the two topics at the top and make notes under each topic. In some cases, you can write an idea about a topic directly across from the related idea on the other side. Look at the example T-chart below listing some arguments for and against being messy.

Arguments for being messy	Arguments against being messy
• Things can be easier to find because they're right out in the open.	• It's easier to lose or misplace the things we need.
• Being messy can help people connect ideas in new ways.	• Being messy can set a bad example for children.

 CATEGORIZE Read and listen to the presentation about the benefits of a happy appearance. Complete the notes in the T-chart on the next page.

ACADEMIC LANGUAGE
It's helpful to listen for key phrases that communicate a contrast. Phrases like *on the other hand, at the same time, rather than,* and *but in fact* tell the listener that contrasting information is coming up.

⌐ OPAL
Oxford Phrasal Academic Lexicon

Sure, we all look better when we smile, but can our facial expressions really cause us to succeed or fail? Many scientists believe that smiling can lead to more success in life, while frowning can lead to more problems. Some researchers discovered that people who smiled in school pictures were more likely to have longer, happier marriages in the future than those who did not. In contrast, people who didn't smile in their class photos tended to get divorced more often. Also, people who smiled in job interviews were more likely to get the jobs than candidates who didn't smile. Smiling also reduces stress, some scientists say. In fact, in one study, smiling while doing a stressful job helped workers' brains and bodies recover from the stress more quickly afterward. On the other hand, people who didn't smile had faster heartbeats long after they finished the stressful job. Maybe this is why smiling can even cause people to live longer. One research study discovered that if baseball players were smiling on their cards, they lived almost seven years longer than players who weren't smiling. So remember to smile!

Happy facial expressions	Serious facial expressions
• longer, happier marriages	• _____
• more likely to get job after an interview	_____
	• _____
• _____	_____
_____	• more stress
• _____	• faster heartbeats after stressful job was finished
_____	

iQ PRACTICE Go online for more practice taking notes using a T-chart.
Practice > Unit 2 > Activity 6

LISTENING 2

Color Schemes: How Colors Make You Buy

OBJECTIVE ▶

You are going to listen to a podcast from the Canadian Broadcasting Company about how a color can be connected with a particular product, both for consumers and in the law. As you listen to the podcast, gather information and ideas about how a color can lead to the success of a product.

PREVIEW THE LISTENING

A. PREVIEW Before you listen, discuss the questions in a small group.

1. Look at the products and logos. Which ones do you recognize? How important is the color of each one? Does it make the product or logo more recognizable?

2. Colors can communicate different meanings. What do these colors communicate to you? Is your response the same as or different from what the color means to North Americans?

RED (EXCITEMENT, BOLDNESS)

ORANGE (FRIENDSHIP, CONFIDENCE)

YELLOW (OPTIMISM, WARMTH)

GREEN (HEALTH, GROWTH)

BLUE (TRUST, STRENGTH)

PURPLE (CREATIVITY, IMAGINATION)

B. VOCABULARY Read aloud these words from Listening 2. Check (✓) the ones you know. Use a dictionary to define any new or unknown words. Then discuss with a partner how the words will relate to the unit.

feature *(n.)* ⚷ OPAL	**manufacture** *(v.)* ⚷	**revert** *(v.)*
grant *(v.)* ⚷	**monopoly** *(n.)* ⚷	**shade** *(n.)* ⚷
imply *(v.)* ⚷ OPAL	**obtain** *(v.)* ⚷ OPAL	**theme** *(n.)* ⚷ OPAL
legal *(adj.)* ⚷ OPAL	**purchase** *(n.)* ⚷	**trademark** *(v.)* ⚷

⚷ Oxford 5000™ words   OPAL Oxford Phrasal Academic Lexicon

iQ PRACTICE Go online to listen and practice your pronunciation.
Practice > Unit 2 > Activity 7

WORK WITH THE LISTENING

🔊 **A. LISTEN AND TAKE NOTES** Listen to the podcast and take notes on the main ideas in the T-chart.

iQ RESOURCES Go online to download extra vocabulary support.
Resources > Extra Vocabulary > Unit 2

Arguments for color branding	Arguments against color branding

B. EXTEND What are other arguments for and against color branding? Write your ideas in the chart above.

🔊 **C. EXPLAIN** Read the questions. Then listen again. Answer the questions. Compare your answers with a partner.

1. How did Owens Corning's insulation become pink?

2. Why did the courts agree that Owens Corning could protect their pink insulation?

3. How are Tiffany's blue boxes and Louboutin's red shoe soles similar?

4. Where did Louboutin get the idea for his red shoe soles?

5. Why did Louboutin sue Yves Saint Laurent?

D. IDENTIFY Listen to sentences from the podcast. Finish the sentences with the details you hear.

1. Owens Corning made the decision to dye their product red in

   _____.

2. Then in _____, Owens Corning made legal history when it became the first company to trademark a single color.

3. According to reports, pink insulation commands over _____ percent of the home insulation market.

4. Christian Louboutin is famous for his glamorous shoe designs that cost anywhere from $_____ to _____.

5. The judge also implied that Louboutin's _____ trademark should be canceled.

E. INTERPRET Read the comments below. Match them with the speaker. Would they have been made by workers at Owens Corning (*OC*), Tiffany (*T*), or Louboutin (*L*)? Match them to the workers who would have said them.

____ 1. "Everyone recognizes our boxes and bags immediately because of the distinct color."

____ 2. "We spent money on marketing and even got the Pink Panther to be our mascot."

____ 3. "Our product isn't very exciting, but our consumers ask for us by our color."

____ 4. "Other companies shouldn't be able to use our color. People connect our shade of red directly to our product."

____ 5. "We disagree with the judge's ruling in the Louboutin court case. If they can't trademark red, then our shade of blue is also in danger!"

____ 6. "We use the same color on the soles of all our products because that is how customers can identify our brand."

F. EXTEND Work with a partner. Imagine you are judges in the court case between Louboutin and Yves Saint Laurent. Complete the T-chart using points from the listening and your own ideas.

Arguments for allowing Louboutin to trademark shoes with red soles	Arguments for allowing Yves Saint Laurent and other companies to sell shoes with red soles

G. DISCUSS Work in a group. Discuss the questions.

1. The podcast asks if a company should be able to "own" a color? What is your opinion? Explain your reasons.

2. What colors do you connect with products? Why do you think the companies might have chosen those particular colors? Would you change any of the color branding?

H. VOCABULARY Here are some words from Listening 2. Complete each sentence with the correct word.

feature *(n.)*	legal *(adj.)*	obtain *(v.)*	shade *(n.)*
grant *(v.)*	manufacture *(v.)*	purchase *(n.)*	theme *(n.)*
imply *(v.)*	monopoly *(n.)*	revert *(v.)*	trademark *(v.)*

1. They _____ cars at the factory down the street.

2. When I don't know a word in English, I often _____ back to my native language.

3. There are laws to keep any one company from getting a _____ of one area of business.

4. I sent in an application to the bank so I can _____ a credit card.

5. After I made my _____, the cashier wrapped it and put it in a bag.

6. The _____ of the party was the 1970s, so everyone was wearing old clothes.

7. The company wants to _____ the product name so no one else can use it.

8. I want the bank to _____ me a $5,000 loan.

9. I don't want to tell him when he is wrong, but I choose my words carefully so I can _____ it.

10. They got _____ advice from their lawyer.

11. The trees are a beautiful _____ of green.

12. An interesting _____ of our city is the waterfront promenade.

a waterfront promenade

iQ PRACTICE Go online for more practice with the vocabulary.
Practice > Unit 2 > Activity 8

WORK WITH THE VIDEO

A. PREVIEW Can you think of any advantages to being messy? Tell a partner.

VIDEO VOCABULARY

tidy (*adj.*) arranged in good order; neat

effciency (*n.*) the ability to work well without wasting time or energy

clutter (*n.*) things that make a place messy

filthy (*adj.*) dirty

iQ RESOURCES Go online to watch the video about the benefits of being messy. *Resources > Video > Unit 2 > Unit Video*

B. IDENTIFY Watch the video two or three times. Check (✓) the benefits according to the video.

____ Messy people are more relaxed and live longer.

____ Being messy saves time.

____ Messy people get more done.

____ Messy people are more reliable than tidy people.

____ People can find things more easily in a messy office.

____ No one likes to be labeled as organized.

____ Messy people tend to be more expressive.

____ Being messy will help you earn more money at your job.

C. CREATE What could a messy person say in response to the following statement? Use the ideas from the video to write a short response that defends being messy.

"Your desk is really messy. How do you get anything done? I couldn't work like this. I like everything to be in its proper place."

SAY WHAT YOU THINK

SYNTHESIZE Think about Listening 1, Listening 2, and the unit video as you discuss the questions.

1. The speakers suggest that the appearance of a product or a space can send a message. What message do you send by your own appearance and the appearance of your possessions?

2. Think about a time that you judged someone based on how he or she looked or organized things. Was your first impression right or wrong? Why?

3. How can colors help a person to be more organized? How could a productive messy person use color to find things more easily?

VOCABULARY SKILL Using the dictionary: words with multiple definitions

When you look a word up in the dictionary, there are often several different **definitions** given. You must consider the context of the word to choose the correct definition.

Decide what part of speech the word is in that context—for example, a *noun* or a *verb*. When you look up the word, you can then quickly eliminate a form or use of the word not appropriate to the context.

> In many places, casual Fridays are starting to **fade**, and there's a move toward "dress-up" or "formal" Thursdays or Mondays.

> **fade** ⚲+ /feɪd/ *verb* **1** [I, T] to become, or to make something become, paler or less bright: *The curtains had faded in the sun.* ◆ **~ from sth** *All color had faded from her face.* ◆ **~ sth** *The sun had faded the curtains.* ◆ *He was wearing faded blue jeans.* **2** [I] to disappear gradually: *Her smile faded.* ◆ **~ away** *Hopes of reaching an agreement seem to be fading away.* ◆ *The laughter faded away.* ◆ **~ to/into sth** *His voice faded to a whisper* (= gradually became quieter). ◆ *All other issues* **fade into insignificance** *compared with the struggle for survival.* **3** [I] if a sports player, team, actor, etc. **fades**, they stop playing or performing as well as they did before: *Black faded on the final bend.* **IDM** see WOODWORK

Read all of the definitions before you make the choice. By thinking about the context of the report, you can conclude that the first definition of *fade* is not correct in this context.

All dictionary entries adapted from the *Oxford Advanced American Dictionary for learners of English* © Oxford University Press 2011.

A. IDENTIFY Read each sentence. Then circle the correct definition of each bold word.

1. Employees were allowed to **ditch** their suits and ties and formal shirts.

> **ditch** /dɪtʃ/ *noun, verb*
> • **noun** a long channel dug at the side of a field or road, to hold or take away water
> • **verb 1** [T] ~ **sth/sb** (*informal*) to get rid of something or someone because you no longer want or need it/them: *The new road building program has been ditched.* **2** [T, I] ~ **(sth)** if a pilot **ditches** an aircraft, or if it **ditches**, it lands in the ocean in an emergency **3** [T] ~ **school** (*informal*) to stay away from school without permission

2. A very neat home can be impersonal and **cold**. A messy house can show your personality.

> **cold** ̇+ /koʊld/ *adj., noun, adv.*
> • **adj.** (cold·er, cold·est)
> > LOW TEMPERATURE **1** having a lower than usual temperature; having a temperature lower than the human body: *I'm cold. Turn the heat up.* ♦ *to **feel/look cold*** ♦ *cold hands and feet* ♦ *a cold room/house* ♦ *Isn't it cold today?* ♦ *It's **freezing cold**.* ♦ *to **get/turn colder*** ♦ ***bitterly cold** weather* ♦ *the coldest May on record*
> > FOOD/DRINKS **2** not heated; cooled after being cooked: *a cold drink* ♦ *Hot and cold food is available in the cafeteria.* ♦ *cold chicken for lunch*
> > UNFRIENDLY **3** (of a person) without emotion; unfriendly: *to give someone a **cold look/stare/welcome*** ♦ *Her manner was **cold and distant**.* ♦ *He was staring at her with **cold eyes**.*

B. APPLY Read each sentence. Then look up the definition of the bold word. Write the correct definition for the context of each bold word.

1. I found out how **deep** the world's bias toward neatness and order is.

   _____

2. The woman received a **fine** of more than two thousand dollars at work.

   _____

3. They're looking for a **sign** that people are professional.

   _____

4. I've been messy since I was old enough to **dress** myself.

   _____

iQ PRACTICE Go online for more practice with using the dictionary to check words with multiple definitions. *Practice > Unit 2 > Activity 9*

SPEAKING

OBJECTIVE ▶ At the end of this unit, you are going to role-play a conversation offering advice to help someone become better organized. You will need to be able to confirm understanding during the conversation.

GRAMMAR Subjunctive for suggestions

The **subjunctive** is the simple or base form of a verb—for example, *go* or *try*.

You can use the subjunctive to make a strong suggestion about something that you think should happen.

A sentence with the subjunctive has two clauses: a main clause and a *that* clause.

In the main clause we use a **suggesting verb** or **suggesting expression**.

In the *that* clause we use the **base form of a verb**.

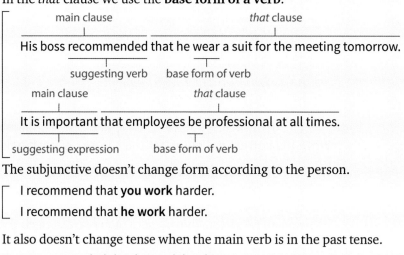

The subjunctive doesn't change form according to the person.

- I recommend that **you work** harder.
- I recommend that **he work** harder.

It also doesn't change tense when the main verb is in the past tense.

- I recommend**ed** that he **work** harder.

To make a negative suggestion, use *not* + the base form of the verb.

- It's essential that employees **not** show up late for meetings.

Certain verbs and certain expressions are often used with the subjunctive to make suggestions and recommendations. The word *that* is optional.

Some verbs followed by the subjunctive	Some expressions followed by the subjunctive
to advise (that)	It's best (that)
to ask (that)	It's desirable (that)
to desire (that)	It's essential (that)
to insist (that)	It's important (that)
to recommend (that)	It's recommended (that)
to request (that)	It's a good idea (that)
to suggest (that)	It's preferred (that)

iQ RESOURCES   Go online to watch the Grammar Skill Video.
Resources > Video > Unit 2 > Grammar Skill Video

A. RESTATE Rewrite the sentences. Use the subjunctive.

1. Customers expect sales reps to dress more formally.

   Customers request that sales reps _____.

2. Employees should try to avoid looking sloppy at work.

   It is recommended that employees _____.

3. When CEOs pose for a work-related photo, they should not wear jeans and sandals.

   When CEOs pose for a work-related photo, it's important that they

   _____.

4. Some executives want their employees to keep their desks clear of personal items.

   Some executives advise that employees _____

   _____.

5. Some experts say that managers should remind their employees to smile more frequently.

   Some experts suggest that managers _____

   _____.

6. I think that people dressing more formally at work is a good idea.

   It's a good idea that people _____.

B. EXTEND Look at the photos. Write advice for each person on how to dress. Use the subjunctive. Then share your advice with a partner.

| A | B |

Photo A: This man just started working in a very formal office.

_____

_____

Photo B: This man is going to start working in a casual office.

_____

_____

iQ PRACTICE Go online for more practice with the subjunctive.
Practice > Unit 2 > Activity 10

iQ PRACTICE Go online for the Grammar Expansion: noun clauses.
Practice > Unit 2 > Activity 11

PRONUNCIATION Unstressed syllables

Vowels in stressed syllables are long and clear. In contrast, vowels in unstressed syllables are often reduced to a short sound called a *schwa* (/ə/). It is the most common vowel sound.

Listen to this word.

 ⌐ appearances

The stressed syllable is the second syllable: *ap-PEAR-an-ces*. The vowel sounds in the unstressed syllables are pronounced /ə/.

⌐ /ə·pɪr·ən·səz/

To make the /ə/ sound, drop your jaw a little and relax your tongue. It is a very short, "lazy" sound.

A. **IDENTIFY** Listen to the words. Which syllables are unstressed? Cross out the unstressed syllables in each word.

TIP FOR SUCCESS

Some online dictionaries have word pronunciations that you can click on. This is a good way to quickly learn the unstressed syllables in new words.

1. pleasure
2. forgotten
3. successful
4. habit

5. business
6. allow
7. cautious
8. professional

 B. **APPLY** Listen again. Repeat the words. Focus on the unstressed syllables.

iQ PRACTICE Go online for more practice with unstressed syllables. *Practice ⟩ Unit 2 ⟩ Activity 12*

 CRITICAL THINKING STRATEGY

Restating information

When you **restate** information, you say something again using different words. Restating helps you to understand information, and it shows you what parts you don't understand. Also, restating information helps you to remember it better, so it's a useful study skill.

Restating is different than summarizing. When you restate, you include the same details as the original, but say them in your own words.

iQ PRACTICE Go online to watch the Critical Thinking Video and check your comprehension. *Practice ⟩ Unit 2 ⟩ Activity 13*

C. **RESTATE** Read the blog. Tell your partner about one of the points by restating the key information.

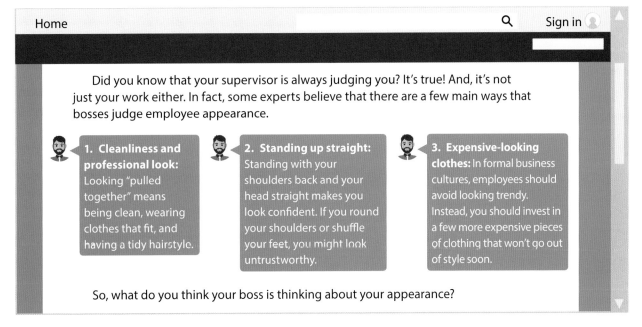

Home   🔍   Sign in

Did you know that your supervisor is always judging you? It's true! And, it's not just your work either. In fact, some experts believe that there are a few main ways that bosses judge employee appearance.

1. Cleanliness and professional look: Looking "pulled together" means being clean, wearing clothes that fit, and having a tidy hairstyle.

2. Standing up straight: Standing with your shoulders back and your head straight makes you look confident. If you round your shoulders or shuffle your feet, you might look untrustworthy.

3. Expensive-looking clothes: In formal business cultures, employees should avoid looking trendy. Instead, you should invest in a few more expensive pieces of clothing that won't go out of style soon.

So, what do you think your boss is thinking about your appearance?

Sometimes you might think that you understand what someone is saying, but you are not exactly sure. These are ways you can check your understanding.

Ask a question that signals your need to confirm your understanding.

Do you mean that . . . ?

Excuse me, are you saying . . . ?

Does that mean . . . ?

Restate what the speaker said in your own words.

If I understand you, . . .

(So) you're saying that . . .

After the speaker responds, let the speaker know that you now understand the information. You can do this by using words or phrases like *thanks, OK, right, I see,* or *got it.*

A. APPLY Listen to the conversations. Complete the conversations using expressions from the Speaking Skill box. Then practice the conversations with a partner.

TIP FOR SUCCESS

Confirming understanding is a great way to participate actively in a conversation. It shows others you are listening and interested.

1. A: Did you hear that the "Made in Britain" logo is changing from blue and red to gray and red?

    B: What? _____ they're not using the colors in the British flag anymore?

    A: Yes. That's what the news said.

    B: Oh.

2. A: More and more customers are looking for a sign of professionalism.

    B: _____ they prefer less casual dress?

    A: Yeah, that's right.

    B: _____ .

3. A: If my desk is too organized, I can't be creative.

    B: _____ , you need to be messy to work well?

    A: Yeah, I need a little mess.

    B: _____ .

4. A: Most people can't get organized all at once.

    B: _____ it's better to work on it step by step?

    A: Yes, it does.

    B: _____ .

B. EXTEND Work in a group. Discuss the questions. Use questions and phrases from the Speaking Skill box to confirm your understanding.

1. What connection is there between appearance and quality of work? Do you think that when people look sloppy, they are less careful at work?

2. Do people's appearance and the condition of their workspace matter if they can get the job done?

3. Do you think that schools should teach students how to be organized?

iQ PRACTICE Go online for more practice confirming understanding. *Practice* ›
Unit 2 › *Activity 14*

UNIT ASSIGNMENT

OBJECTIVE ▶

Role-play a conversation

In this assignment, you are going to role-play a conversation offering advice to help someone become better organized. As you prepare your role-play, think about the Unit Question, "How does appearance affect our success?" Use information from Listening 1, Listening 2, the unit video, and your work in this unit to support your role-play. Refer to the Self-Assessment checklist on page 50.

CONSIDER THE IDEAS

In a group, list situations that can create a mess at school or work (e.g., piles of paper, not enough storage space). Discuss ways to make the situations better.

PREPARE AND SPEAK

A. GATHER IDEAS Imagine you are in a business to help clients get organized. Read about a new client. Take notes on his situation. Create a T-chart with two columns labeled *Problems* and *Details*.

Name: Dan Howard

Occupation: Sales representative

The Situation: A few years ago, I had the best sales record in my department. My customers respected me, and they were loyal to me. In the past couple of years, however, my sales have dropped. I was doing OK until my manager moved me into a smaller office. There is less storage space for my paperwork. Now I can't find anything. I have piles of customers' papers everywhere. I even lost my phone last week. My old customers don't ask for my help anymore. The few new customers I have don't seem to trust me. I can't blame them. I can't find anything they need. My sales are now the worst in my department. I need help!

B. ORGANIZE IDEAS What advice would you offer to help Dan Howard? Write notes about two or three pieces of advice you would give him. Give details and examples to support your advice.

Advice to improve the situation	Details and examples

C. SPEAK Role-play a conversation with a partner. One person gives advice using the subjunctive when appropriate. The other person role-plays Dan Howard and should confirm understanding. Present the role-play to the class. Refer to the Self-Assessment checklist below before you begin.

iQ PRACTICE Go online for your alternate Unit Assignment.
Practice > Unit 2 > Activity 15

CHECK AND REFLECT

A. CHECK Think about the Unit Assignment as you complete the Self-Assessment checklist.

SELF-ASSESSMENT	Yes	No
I was able to speak easily about the topic.	☐	☐
My partner, group, and class understood me.	☐	☐
I used a T-chart to take notes.	☐	☐
I used the subjunctive.	☐	☐
I used vocabulary from the unit.	☐	☐
I confirmed understanding.	☐	☐
I pronounced unstressed syllables correctly.	☐	☐

B. REFLECT Discuss these questions with a partner or group.

1. What is something new you learned in this unit?

2. Look back at the Unit Question—How does appearance affect our success? Is your answer different now than when you started this unit? If yes, how is it different? Why?

iQ PRACTICE Go to the online discussion board to discuss the questions.
Practice > Unit 2 > Activity 16

TRACK YOUR SUCCESS

iQ PRACTICE Go online to check the words and phrases you have learned in this unit. *Practice > Unit 2 > Activity 17*

Check (✓) the skills and strategies you learned. If you need more work on a skill, refer to the page(s) in parentheses.

LISTENING	☐ I can identify details. (p. 33)
NOTE-TAKING	☐ I can take notes using a T-chart. (p. 34)
VOCABULARY	☐ I can use the dictionary to find multiple definitions of a word. (p. 42)
GRAMMAR	☐ I can use the subjunctive for suggestions. (p. 44)
PRONUNCIATION	☐ I can pronounce unstressed syllables correctly. (p. 46)
CRITICAL THINKING	☐ I can restate information. (p. 47)
SPEAKING	☐ I can confirm understanding. (p. 48)

OBJECTIVE ▶ ☐ I can gather information and ideas to role-play a conversation offering advice to help someone become better organized.

Developmental Psychology

NOTE-TAKING	taking notes using key words and phrases
LISTENING	making predictions
CRITICAL THINKING	assessing predictions
VOCABULARY	using the dictionary: words with similar meanings
GRAMMAR	phrasal verbs
PRONUNCIATION	sentence stress
SPEAKING	giving a presentation

What skills make someone an adult?

A. Discuss these questions with your classmates.

1. In your opinion, at what age does a person become an adult? Why?

2. What important events or experiences can make you feel more like an adult?

3. Look at the photo. What is the woman doing? How does this make her an adult?

B. Listen to *The Q Classroom* online. Then answer these questions.

1. What skills do Felix and Sophy give as examples of adult behavior? Do you agree with them?

2. Marcus recalls a specific event as a turning point between childhood and adulthood. What kinds of skills are involved in hosting a family dinner? How are those skills related to being an adult?

iQ PRACTICE Go to the online discussion board to discuss the Unit Question with your classmates. *Practice > Unit 3 > Activity 1*

UNIT OBJECTIVE ➤ Listen to a lecture, watch a video, and listen to a podcast and gather information and ideas to present a personal story.

NOTE-TAKING SKILL Taking notes using key words and phrases

You can't write down every word as you listen to a lecture or presentation. Speakers may talk too quickly or say things that are not essential to their message. When you take notes, quickly decide which words are important and which words aren't. Write the key words and phrases in your notes.

Here are some tips to help you identify key words and phrases:

- They are directly connected to the topic.
- They communicate the main idea and important supporting details.
- They are usually repeated or rephrased.
- They may be specific names, dates, places, or events.

Do not try to write complete sentences in your notes. Key words and phrases are all you need to help you summarize what you heard.

A. IDENTIFY Listen to the presentation about two ceremonies that celebrate becoming an adult. Check (✓) the key words and phrases. Compare your answers with a partner and explain why you have chosen them.

Ceremony 1	Ceremony 2
☐ very interesting	☐ one tradition
☐ Japan	☐ still popular
☐ special	☐ *Quinceañera*
☐ national holiday	☐ Mexico
☐ second Monday in January	☐ girls
☐ *Seijin no Hi*	☐ celebrate
☐ many young men and women	☐ fifteenth birthday
☐ twenty years old	☐ long, formal dresses
☐ traditional clothes	☐ party
☐ ceremony at government office	☐ dance with their fathers
☐ attend parties with friends	☐ different cultures

B. SUMMARIZE Use your own words to summarize one of the ceremonies discussed in Activity A.

iQ PRACTICE Go online for more practice taking notes using key words and phrases. *Practice > Unit 3 > Activity 2*

Seijin no Hi

Quinceañera

LISTENING 1

OBJECTIVE ▶

"Adulting" School

You are going to listen to a lecture and watch a video news report about a school that teaches young people skills normally associated with being an adult. As you listen to the lecture and watch the video, gather information and ideas about what skills make someone an adult.

PREVIEW THE LISTENING

A. PREVIEW You are going to listen to a lecture about a specific group of adults who don't have a set of skills. Before you listen, discuss the questions in a small group.

1. Look at the names of different generations. Match the names with the years people in each generation were probably born.

Generation X	1920s to 1940s
Generation Z	1940s to 1960s
The Silent Generation	1960s to 1980s
Millennials	1980s to early 2000s
The Baby Boomers	early 2000s to now

2. Which generation do you belong to? What do you know about the characteristics and values of your generation?

B. VOCABULARY Read aloud these words from Listening 1. Check (✓) the ones you know. Use a dictionary to define any new or unknown words. Then discuss with a partner how the words will relate to the unit.

debt *(n.)* ℞	minor *(adj.)* ℞ OPAL	set up *(v. phr.)* ℞
entrepreneur *(n.)* ℞	nutrition *(n.)* ℞	spare *(n.)*
insurance *(n.)* ℞	precisely *(adv.)* ℞ OPAL	weigh in *(v. phr.)*
interest *(n.)* ℞ OPAL	retirement *(n.)* ℞	

℞ Oxford 5000™ words   **OPAL** Oxford Phrasal Academic Lexicon

iQ PRACTICE Go online to listen and practice your pronunciation.
Practice > Unit 3 > Activity 3

WORK WITH THE LISTENING

iQ RESOURCES Go online to watch the video.
Resources > Video > Unit 3 > Listening 1

A. LISTEN AND TAKE NOTES Listen to the lecture. Then watch the video.* Complete the chart with the main points of the lecture and video. Write down only the important words. Compare your notes with a partner.

iQ RESOURCES Go online to download extra vocabulary support.
Resources > Extra Vocabulary > Unit 3

Main ideas	Details
"Adulting" skills—examples?	
How previously learned?	
What is "Adulting" School?	
Why does this appeal to Millennials?	

*Audio version available. Resources > Audio > Unit 3

B. IDENTIFY Listen and watch again. Check (✓) the "adulting" skills that the lecture and the video say Millennials might need to learn.

____ 1. searching for a job   ____ 6. repairing clothing

____ 2. giving a strong handshake   ____ 7. folding a sheet

____ 3. time management   ____ 8. how to pay back student debt

____ 4. minor car repairs   ____ 9. speaking a second language

____ 5. buying a home   ____10. giving a speech

C. CATEGORIZE Read the comments about the "Adulting" School. Match each quote with the speaker who probably said it. Compare your answers with a partner.

a. Rachel Weinstein: one of the founders of the "Adulting" School

b. A student at the "Adulting" School

c. A teacher at the "Adulting" School

____ 1. "It's really satisfying to share the basic cooking skills I learned from my mother and grandmother when I was young with a new generation."

____ 2. "I saw an advertisement for an insurance company that offered to teach insurance basics to its customers, and it gave me a great idea that I couldn't wait to share with my friend."

____ 3. "I really want to feel confident when I have to make financial decisions, and I just don't right now. My school didn't offer any classes in budgeting or anything like that."

____ 4. "I know I could watch a video online about some of these things, but it's really great to have a teacher. I can ask questions and post questions in a chat room or by email."

____ 5. "It can be really helpful to know how to take care of your car. I have always saved a lot of money by being able to do some simple things on my own. It's not hard to learn, and I love seeing students' confidence increase."

D. CATEGORIZE Read the statements. Write *T* (true) or *F* (false). Then correct each false statement to make it true.

_____ 1. Millennials are often comfortable with digital technologies.

_____ 2. Older people understand why Millennials might want to take "adulting" lessons.

_____ 3. The entrepreneurs who started the "Adulting" School teach in a very serious manner.

_____ 4. Millennials don't always understand everything associated with paying back a loan.

_____ 5. Millennials may have been encouraged to think creatively but not practically.

E. VOCABULARY Here are some words from Listening 1. Complete each sentence with the correct word.

debt *(n.)*	interest *(n.)*	precisely *(adv.)*	spare *(n.)*
entrepreneur *(n.)*	minor *(adj.)*	retirement *(n.)*	weigh in *(v. phr.)*
insurance *(n.)*	nutrition *(n.)*	set up *(v. phr.)*	

1. They looked _____ the same to me.

2. I like my parents to _____ on some decisions before I make them. I find their opinions helpful.

3. I lost my key, so I need to use my _____ to unlock the door.

4. I didn't tell them because it was really a _____ problem. It wasn't serious at all.

5. I need to pay off my _____ to the store. I owe $100.

6. The company was started by two young _____.

7. His dream is to _____ his own business.

8. I don't like to borrow money because I hate to pay all the _____.

9. Good _____ is an important part of a healthy lifestyle.

10. The car was damaged in the accident, but we have _____ that will pay for the repairs.

11. At 60, he will soon be approaching _____ age.

iQ PRACTICE   Go online for more practice with the vocabulary.
Practice > Unit 3 > Activity 4

iQ PRACTICE   Go online for additional listening and comprehension.
Practice > Unit 3 > Activity 5

SAY WHAT YOU THINK

DISCUSS Work in a group to discuss the questions.

1. What are the skills from Listening 1 that you associate with adulthood? Can you think of any others that were not mentioned?

2. Can you remember an event or experience that made you feel like you had become an adult? What skills did you need at that time?

LISTENING SKILL Making predictions

Predictions are guesses you make based only on the information that is available. For example, you may know the title of a lecture. You can use the title to predict the topic and the ideas it might cover.

Your predictions are also based on what you already know about a topic. Background information from articles you have read, from electronic media, and from previous experiences all help prepare you to understand new information, and to predict what you are likely to hear next.

One way to make predictions is to write down the topic. Then take brief notes on the ideas and vocabulary you already know that are associated with that topic. This prepares you for the information that you will hear, so you don't have to work quite as hard to understand it.

TIP FOR SUCCESS

Graphic organizers work well for making predictions. Web diagrams are very useful. Write the topic in a circle in the center. Write notes about your predictions and possible vocabulary on lines coming from the center.

A. APPLY Read the lecture titles. Predict the topic of the lecture and the main ideas it might cover. Write brief notes about what you already know about each topic. Then list five words you might expect to hear about it.

1. Trends in World Architecture (*Architecture Appreciation Lecture*)

2. Global Warming (*Environmental Studies*)

3. Technology in Schools (*Media Studies*)

B. IDENTIFY Read the questions. Then listen to the excerpts. Circle the correct answers.

1. Which of the following is most likely to be discussed in the lecture?

   a. what to do when you want a promotion

   b. how to explain your side of an argument

   c. what kinds of jobs are right for you

2. What is Adam most likely to suggest?

   a. Don't take the online class that I took.

   b. You should focus on your job.

   c. Schedule some time every night just for homework.

3. What is Tara most likely to say next?

   a. "You're going to have a wonderful time."

   b. "You still owe me some money."

   c. "You were never very nice to me."

4. How will the employees most likely feel when they hear the news?

   a. worried

   b. confused

   c. excited

iQ PRACTICE Go online for more practice listening to make predictions. *Practice > Unit 3 > Activity 6*

CRITICAL THINKING STRATEGY

Assessing predictions

While making predictions is a useful listening skill, it's important not only to make the predictions but also to assess how accurate your predictions are so you can make better predictions moving forward. Here are helpful steps for assessing your predictions:

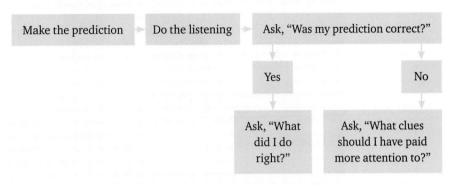

iQ PRACTICE Go online to watch the Critical Thinking Video and check your comprehension. *Practice > Unit 3 > Activity 7*

C. **IDENTIFY** Work with a partner. Look at the lecture title. Predict the main ideas it might cover. Then listen to the beginning of the lecture. Circle the ideas that you correctly predicted.

Water Shortages: The Causes of a Global Crisis (Geography Lecture)

What I think the main ideas might be: _____

_____

_____

D. **ANALYZE** Discuss these questions about your predictions in Activity C.

1. How did you correctly guess the main ideas?

2. Why were some of your guesses incorrect?

E. **ANALYZE** Look back at your predictions in Activity A on page 59. Look at the main ideas you thought you might hear. Circle the ones that were in the lectures. Then ask yourself what you did right and how you can make better predictions in the future.

Financial Literacy Among Young People

OBJECTIVE ▶

You are going to listen to a podcast from the Canadian Broadcasting Company about financial knowledge among young people. As you listen to the podcast, gather information and ideas about what skills make someone an adult.

PREVIEW THE LISTENING

A. PREVIEW Before you listen, read the title of the podcast and look at the photo above. What predictions can you make about what the speaker might say? Discuss your ideas with a partner.

B. VOCABULARY Read aloud these words from Listening 2. Check (✓) the ones you know. Use a dictionary to define any new or unknown words. Then discuss with a partner how the words will relate to the unit.

agency *(n.)* 🔑	mortgage *(n.)* 🔑	stock *(n.)* 🔑 OPAL
asset *(n.)* 🔑	naturally *(adv.)* 🔑 OPAL	tool *(n.)* 🔑 OPAL
balance *(v.)* 🔑 OPAL	pension *(n.)* 🔑	tedious *(adj.)*
current *(adj.)* 🔑 OPAL	series *(n.)* 🔑 OPAL	truly *(adv.)* 🔑

🔑 Oxford 5000™ words   OPAL Oxford Phrasal Academic Lexicon

iQ PRACTICE Go online to listen and practice your pronunciation.
Practice > Unit 3 > Activity 8

WORK WITH THE LISTENING

 A. LISTEN AND TAKE NOTES Listen to the podcast and read the notes. Cross out the words that are not important. Compare your answers with a partner.

iQ RESOURCES Go online to download extra vocabulary support.
Resources > Extra Vocabulary > Unit 3

A man and woman went to the bank to get a mortgage.

The banker talked about a lot of financial things.

The man fell asleep.

The man was bored because he was financially illiterate.

The man doesn't understand the first thing about finances.

Forbes magazine reported that teenagers are dangerously financially

   illiterate.

It is killing us.

Young people don't know the difference between an asset and a liability.

This is happening in the US and in Canada.

The government in Canada started the Financial Consumer Agency of

   Canada in 2001.

Its job is to teach young people about finances.

It has a month—November—to promote financial literacy.

Schools in Ontario have started to talk about money to children in

   elementary school.

B. APPLY Use your notes to summarize the main ideas of the podcast. Complete the sentences.

1. Many young people _____.

2. The solution to the problem seems to be _____.

C. ANALYZE Think about your predictions from Activity A on page 59. Were any of your predictions correct? If so, how did you make those predictions? What will help you make better predictions in the future?

D. CATEGORIZE Read the statements. Then listen again. Write *T* (true) or *F* (false). Then correct each false statement to make it true.

_____ 1. Banks make the speaker feel relaxed.

_____ 2. *Forbes* magazine is worried about the state of financial literacy among young people.

_____ 3. Students remember financial literacy lessons for about two years.

_____ 4. The speaker had a savings account when he was a child where he saved his allowance.

_____ 5. The speaker's dream salary was $100,000.

_____ 6. The Financial Consumer Agency of Canada's only job is to teach young people about finances.

_____ 7. The Financial Consumer Agency of Canada thinks financial literacy is important.

_____ 8. The speaker is sure he would be financially literate if he had studied finances when he was young.

E. CATEGORIZE Read about some choices young people made. Do they seem financially literate or financially illiterate? Write *L* for financially literate and *I* for financially illiterate. Compare answers with a partner.

_____ 1. "I got a really big student loan so I could quit my job and relax more between classes. I'll pay it back someday when I get a really good job. I'm not worried at all."

_____ 2. "The bank offered us a really big mortgage, but we wanted to make sure we could afford the monthly payments without changing our lifestyle. We actually borrowed less money than the bank offered."

_____ 3. "I earn a pretty good paycheck, and I like to shop and have fun. I don't usually save money because somehow it's just all gone by the time I get paid again."

_____ 4. "I am too busy to make a financial retirement plan for my future. I am sure things will work out OK. I will have children, and they will take care of me. I don't need to think about it now."

_____ 5. "I try to pay off my credit card debt every month. I really don't like to owe money, and I hate paying interest. It's like throwing money into the garbage can."

_____ 6. "I want to buy a new smartphone, but I don't have enough money right now. I'm going to save some money each month, and in a few months, I'll have enough."

F. DISCUSS Work in groups to discuss the questions.

1. Were you surprised to hear that financial illiteracy is so high among young people? Why or why not?

2. Think about your own financial literacy. What do you know about? Circle the topics you feel confident talking about.

buying a house	investments	repaying a loan
credit cards	making a budget	retirement savings
credit scores	making smart purchases	saving for emergencies
insurance		

G. VOCABULARY Here are some words from Listening 2. Read the sentences. Then write each bold word next to the correct definition.

1. It was a **truly** wonderful evening.

2. He works for the government at the Environmental Protection **Agency**.

3. We took out for a **mortgage** to buy our new house.

4. When he retired from work at 65 years old, he started to receive a **pension**.

5. If you don't **balance** your finances by doing a budget every month, you might be spending more than you are earning.

6. She makes a financial plan for each year, and now she is working on a budget for the **current** year.

7. The computer is a valuable **tool** used by almost every profession.

8. The school is offering a **series** of classes on financial literacy. You can sign up for all of them now or one at a time.

9. A strong runner is an **asset** to a football team.

10. **Naturally**, I get upset when things go wrong.

11. I wish I had bought **stocks** in Apple when they were first offered. I would be really rich now.

12. I find sewing to be very **tedious** work. It's dull and too detailed for me.

a. _____ (*v.*) to show that in a bank account the total money spent is equal to the total money received

b. _____ (*adj.*) boring

c. _____ (*n.*) a thing that helps you to do your job or to achieve something

d. _____ (*n.*) money paid regularly by a government or company to somebody who is considered to be too old or too ill/sick to work

e. _____ (*adj.*) of the present time

f. _____ (*adv.*) in a way that you would expect

g. _____ (*adv.*) used to emphasize a particular quality

h. _____ (*n.*) a person or thing that is valuable

i. _____ (*n.*) a government department that provides a particular service

j. _____ (n.) several events or things of a similar kind that happen one after the other

k. _____ (n.) a legal agreement by which a bank or similar organization lends you money to buy a house and you pay the money back over a particular number of years

l. _____ (n.) a share that somebody has bought in a company or business

iQ PRACTICE Go online for more practice with the vocabulary.
Practice > Unit 3 > Activity 9

SAY WHAT YOU THINK

SYNTHESIZE Think about Listening 1 and Listening 2 as you discuss the questions.

1. Who should be responsible for teaching young people important life skills? Their parents? Schools? The government? Private institutions?

2. Do you think these skills really make someone a successful adult? If yes, why? If no, what skills might be more important?

VOCABULARY SKILL Using the dictionary: words with similar meanings

There are many words that have similar meanings but are not exactly the same. For example, both *adolescence* and *youth* can be used for the time between childhood and adulthood. Read the following definitions.

> **ad·o·les·cence** /ˌædlˈɛsns/ *noun* [U] the time in a person's life when he or she develops from a child into an adult
> **SYN** PUBERTY ⊃ collocations at AGE

> **youth** ⏚+ /yuθ/ *noun* (*pl.* **youths** /yuðz; yuθs/) **1** [U] the time of life when a person is young, especially the time before a child becomes an adult.

The dictionary definitions show that although the words are very similar, *adolescence* describes a more specific time period, while *youth* is more general.

Checking the definitions of similar words can help you determine which word is appropriate in a context.

All dictionary entries adapted from the *Oxford Advanced American Dictionary for learners of English* © Oxford University Press 2011.

A. APPLY Read the dictionary definitions of words from this unit and their synonyms. Complete each sentence with the correct word.

1. a. If you are having trouble managing your money, you should go to the bank

    to get some _____ advice.

    b. Countries such as India and China have experienced rapid

    _____ growth in recent years.

---

ec·o·nom·ic 🔊+ ⭕ /ˌɛkəˈnɑmɪk; ˌikə-/ *adj.*
1 [only before noun] connected with the trade, industry, and development of wealth of a country, an area, or a society: *social, economic and political issues*

fi·nan·cial 🔊+ Ⓦ /fəˈnænʃl; faɪ-/ *adj.* [usually before noun]
connected with money and finance: *financial services* ◆ *to give financial advice* ◆ *to be in **financial difficulties***

---

2. a. The lawyer can _____ that the man is guilty of the crime by

    recreating the events of the day.

    b. The report _____ us that there is still a lot of work to do.

---

dem·on·strate 🔊+ Ⓦ /ˈdɛmənˌstreɪt/ *verb*
1 [T] to show something clearly by giving proof or evidence: **~ that**...*These results demonstrate convincingly that our campaign is working.* ◆ **~ sth (to sb)** *Let me demonstrate to you some of the difficulties we are facing.*

show 🔊+ ⭕ /ʃoʊ/ *verb, noun*
• *verb* (showed, shown /ʃoʊn/ or, rarely, showed)
> MAKE CLEAR **1** [T] to make something clear; to prove something: **~ (that)**...*The figures clearly show that her claims are false.* ◆ **~ sb that**... *Market research has shown us that people want quality, not just low prices.* ◆ **~ sth**... *a report showing*

B. COMPOSE Look up the definitions of these pairs of words. Write an appropriate sentence using each word. Take turns reading your sentences to a partner.

1. assume / suppose (*v.*)

2. age / mature (*v.*)

3. response / reply (*n.*)

4. order / instruct (*v.*)

5. cover / hide (*v.*)

iQ PRACTICE   Go online for more practice using the dictionary to check words with similar meanings. *Practice > Unit 3 > Activity 10*

SPEAKING

At the end of this unit, you are going to present a personal story describing an important event in your life that made you feel like an adult. In order to tell your story, you will need to follow the appropriate steps for giving a presentation.

GRAMMAR Phrasal verbs

Phrasal verbs are verbs that consist of two words used together. The first word is a verb and the second word is called a *particle*. Particles sometimes look like prepositions, but they have different meanings. The verb and the particle together make a new meaning. For example, *take on* is a phrasal verb. When you put the words *take* and *on* together, they mean "to accept."

> He **took on** a lot of responsibilities.

There are two kinds of phrasal verbs: *transitive* and *intransitive*.

Transitive Phrasal Verbs

A transitive phrasal verb requires a direct object.

> He **picked up** his brother from school.
> verb particle object

Most transitive phrasal verbs are *separable*. This means the direct object can also go between the verb and the particle.

> He **picked** his brother **up** from school.
> verb object particle

When the direct object is a pronoun, it must go between the verb and the particle.

> ✓ He **picked** <u>him</u> **up** from school.
> ✗ He **picked up** <u>him</u> from school.

Some transitive phrasal verbs are inseparable. This means the direct object cannot go between the verb and the particle.

> ✓ My mother is busy today, so I'll **look after** the baby.
> ✗ My mother is busy today, so I'll **look** the baby **after**.

Intransitive Phrasal Verbs

Intransitive phrasal verbs don't take a direct object at all. They are never separable.

> In some situations, children **grow up** faster than in others.

It can be difficult to understand the meaning of a phrasal verb by looking at the words that make it up. Also, some phrasal verbs have more than one meaning. When you learn a new phrasal verb's meaning, you must also learn if it is transitive or intransitive and whether it is separable or inseparable.

iQ RESOURCES Go online to watch the Grammar Skill Video.
Resources > Video > Unit 3 > Grammar Skill Video

A. IDENTIFY Listen to the sentences with phrasal verbs. Write the particles you hear.

1. grow _____

2. weigh _____

3. pay _____

4. sneak education _____

5. figure it _____

6. drop _____ on

TIP FOR SUCCESS

In the dictionary, phrasal verbs are usually located with the definition(s) of the verb in the phrasal verb. Many dictionaries also have example sentences that follow the definitions. Example sentences are an easy way to see if a phrasal verb is *transitive* or *intransitive* and *separable* or *inseparable*.

B. CATEGORIZE Read the sentences. Underline each phrasal verb. Write *T* (transitive) or *I* (intransitive).

____ 1. I don't know what to do about this problem, but we need to work it out.

____ 2. I waved goodbye to my parents and got on a plane.

____ 3. Lessons about financial literacy are going on all over Canada these days.

____ 4. Many children all over the world have to give their childhoods up early and go to work.

____ 5. Adults need to know how to take care of living things like pets or plants and ultimately maybe children.

____ 6. Being an adult means getting out of bed when your baby is crying even when you are really tired.

iQ PRACTICE Go online for more practice with phrasal verbs.
Practice > Unit 3 > Activity 11

iQ PRACTICE Go online for the Grammar Expansion: phrasal verbs with different meanings. *Practice > Unit 3 > Activity 12*

PRONUNCIATION Sentence stress

Words in a sentence are not pronounced with equal stress. Words that contain important information, called **content words**, are said with more stress. They are longer, louder, higher pitched, and clearer. Words that serve a grammatical purpose are called **function words**. They are usually unstressed.

Stressing words focuses the listener's attention on the most important ideas in sentences. Using sentence stress correctly makes it easier to communicate your ideas.

Content words: usually stressed		Function words: usually unstressed	
Nouns	father, Tuesday, etc.	**Articles**	a, an, the
Main verbs	come, walks, etc.	**Auxiliary verbs**	be, have, can, etc.
Adjectives	beautiful, red, etc.	**Prepositions**	in, at, etc.
Adverbs	quickly, very, etc.	**Personal pronouns**	I, you, me, etc.
Negatives	not, can't, etc.	**Possessive pronouns**	my, your, his, etc.
Question words	where, how, etc.	**Relative pronouns**	that, which, who, etc.
Demonstrative pronouns	this, that, etc.	**Short connector words**	and, so, when, then, etc.

For example, listen to the following sentence. The underlined words are stressed.

🔊 ☐ I <u>became</u> an <u>adult</u> when I got <u>married</u> and <u>started</u> a <u>family</u>.

🔊 **A. ANALYZE** Listen to the sentences. Underline the stressed words you hear. Then practice saying the sentences with a partner.

1. When you become employed, you can call yourself an adult.

2. I think it's how much you can provide for yourself.

3. I think it's when you get married.

4. I think you become an adult at 16.

5. The day that I'm an adult is the day that I can do whatever I want to do.

6. The age at which you become an adult varies.

B. CATEGORIZE Underline the important content words in the conversation. Then work with a partner to read the conversation. Stress the content words.

A: Congratulations!

B: Thanks! I can't believe I've graduated already.

A: Yeah. You're an adult now!

B: But I don't feel like an adult. I don't think I learned the right skills in school.

A: Really? Well, I have been taking care of my younger siblings for years now, and I learned a lot of things the hard way.

B: I still rely on my parents a lot.

A: Well, maybe that will change now that you've graduated!

iQ PRACTICE Go online for more practice with sentence stress.
Practice › Unit 3 › Activity 13

SPEAKING SKILL Giving a presentation

When you give a presentation, it is important to look and feel confident. People will be more interested in your ideas if they see that you believe in yourself and your ideas. Here are some steps to follow.

Before you give your presentation

1. Make sure you can clearly pronounce all the key words in your speech. Concentrate on proper word stress.

2. Make sure your notes are well organized. Memorize the main points of your speech so that you won't need to read your presentation. You want to look at your audience, not down at your notes.

3. Practice your presentation several times. Practice in front of a mirror and in front of a friend or family member.

When you begin your presentation

1. Introduce yourself clearly and confidently.

2. Remember to smile.

During your presentation

1. Make eye contact with members of the audience. You want them to feel you want to communicate with each of them.

2. Think about your hand gestures and posture as you speak. You want to appear relaxed and in control. If you move too much, or too little, you will appear nervous. Use gestures for emphasis and to make your points clearer.

A. CREATE Listen to a presentation about becoming an adult. Then list five suggestions you would give the speaker. Compare your suggestions with a partner.

Suggestions:

1. _____

   _____

2. _____

   _____

3. _____

   _____

4. _____

   _____

5. _____

   _____

B. SYNTHESIZE Create a brief presentation to tell about one important event in your life. Practice the presentation once and then present it to a partner. Take note of the suggestions your partner gives you. Take turns presenting and giving suggestions.

iQ PRACTICE Go online for more practice giving a presentation.
Practice > Unit 3 > Activity 14

Give a presentation to a group

OBJECTIVE ▶

In this section, you will give a short presentation about a personal story. As you prepare your presentation, think about the Unit Question, "What skills make someone an adult"? Use information from Listening 1, Listening 2, and your work in this unit to support your presentation. Refer to the Self-Assessment checklist on page 76.

CONSIDER THE IDEAS

 A. LISTEN AND TAKE NOTES Listen to one person's story about a skill he had to learn as he became an adult. Take notes as you listen.

1. What important event became a turning point in the speaker's life?	
2. What dream did the speaker give up?	
3. What skill did he learn that made him feel more grown up?	

B. DISCUSS Work with a partner. Compare your notes and discuss the speaker's main points.

PREPARE AND SPEAK

TIP FOR SUCCESS
When you are brainstorming, no idea is a bad idea. Write down any ideas you have.

A. GATHER IDEAS Brainstorm about important skills you gained that made you feel more like an adult. Make notes in the spider map.

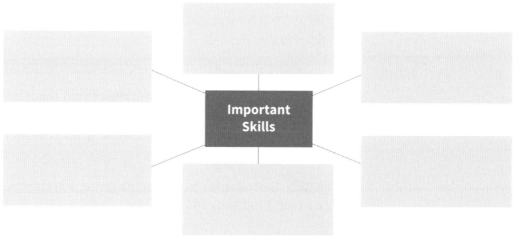

B. ORGANIZE IDEAS Complete these activities.

1. Choose one event to use for your presentation.

2. Use the chart to organize your ideas. It is not necessary to write full sentences. Just write notes. Try to include some phrasal verbs in your presentation.

Introduction (main idea)

Important ideas and details

Conclusion

3. Work with a partner to practice your presentation until you can answer *yes* to the following questions.

   a. Did you introduce yourself clearly?

   b. Did you pronounce all the key words correctly?

   c. Did you use stress correctly?

   d. Did you use your notes to tell your ideas rather than read them?

   e. Did you make eye contact?

   f. Did you use relaxed gestures?

   g. Did you smile?

C. SPEAK Present your personal story. Follow these steps. Refer to the Self-Assessment checklist below before you begin.

1. Work in a group. Take turns presenting your personal stories.

2. Pay attention to how your classmates make their presentations. Try to make predictions about what they will say. Offer suggestions to group members when they complete their presentations.

iQ PRACTICE Go online for your alternate Unit Assignment.
Practice > Unit 3 > Activity 15

CHECK AND REFLECT

A. CHECK Think about the Unit Assignment as you complete the Self-Assessment checklist.

SELF-ASSESSMENT	Yes	No
I was able to speak easily about the topic.	☐	☐
I took notes using key words and phrases.	☐	☐
My partner, group, and class understood me.	☐	☐
I made predictions about the presentations.	☐	☐
I used vocabulary from the unit.	☐	☐
I gave a presentation.	☐	☐
I used sentence stress correctly.	☐	☐

B. REFLECT Discuss these questions with a partner or group.

1. What is something new you learned in this unit?

2. Look back at the Unit Question—What skills make someone an adult? Is your answer different now than when you started this unit? If yes, how is it different? Why?

iQ PRACTICE Go to the online discussion board to discuss the questions.
Practice > Unit 3 > Activity 16

TRACK YOUR SUCCESS

iQ PRACTICE Go online to check the words and phrases you have learned in this unit. *Practice > Unit 3 > Activity 17*

Check (✓) the skills and strategies you learned. If you need more work on a skill, refer to the page(s) in parentheses.

NOTE-TAKING	☐ I can take notes using key words and phrases. (p. 54)
LISTENING	☐ I can make predictions. (p. 59)
CRITICAL THINKING	☐ I can assess my predictions for accuracy. (p. 61)
VOCABULARY	☐ I can use the dictionary to check the definitions of words with similar meanings to fit a context. (p. 67)
GRAMMAR	☐ I can use phrasal verbs. (p. 69)
PRONUNCIATION	☐ I can use appropriate sentence stress. (p. 71)
SPEAKING	☐ I can give a presentation. (p. 72)

OBJECTIVE ▶ ☐ I can gather information and ideas to present a personal story describing an important event in my life.

Science

4

NOTE-TAKING	using a split page
LISTENING	making inferences
VOCABULARY	word forms
CRITICAL THINKING	distinguishing between similar words
GRAMMAR	present perfect and present perfect continuous
PRONUNCIATION	basic intonation patterns
SPEAKING	avoiding answering questions

How do the laws of science affect our lives?

A. Discuss these questions with your classmates.

1. Which science subject did you like best in school: biology, chemistry, or physics? Why?

2. The laws of science describe natural events. What laws of science do you know about?

3. Look at the photo. When a rocket is launched, it demonstrates Newton's third law of motion. What do you think that law says?

B. Listen to *The Q Classroom* online. Then match the laws in the box with the students who talked about them.

a. Archimedes's buoyancy principle
b. Newton's law of gravitation
c. Newton's third law of motion

Marcus	
Sophy	
Yuna	
Felix	

iQ PRACTICE Go to the online discussion board to discuss the Unit Question with your classmates. *Practice > Unit 4 > Activity 1*

UNIT OBJECTIVE

Listen to a class discussion, watch a video, and listen to a lecture. Gather information and ideas to create a role-play about presenting a business plan for a new product.

Using a split-page method to take notes can help you better understand and remember information. To use the split-page method, divide your page into two sections by folding it lengthwise. Write your notes about main ideas and important details in the section on the right. After you have listened, read your notes and write questions about what you heard in the section on the left. You can write questions that are answered in your notes, questions you think might be asked on a quiz or test, or questions you would like to find answers to.

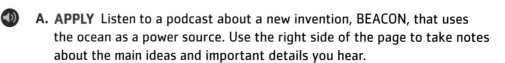

| Questions | Notes on main ideas and important details |

A. APPLY Listen to a podcast about a new invention, BEACON, that uses the ocean as a power source. Use the right side of the page to take notes about the main ideas and important details you hear.

Hannah Herbst and BEACON

Questions	Notes on main ideas and important details
	_____—Hannah Herbst
	_____—Bringing Electricity
	Access to Countries through Ocean Energy
	Appearance: _____
	_____
	_____
	What it does: _____
	_____
	Hydropower—Newton's _____
	When _____ hit the
	_____, they move.
	When the _____ move,
	they make a generator turn, which makes
	_____.

B. COMPOSE Review your notes from Activity A. Write questions about the notes in the section on the left.

iQ PRACTICE Go online for more practice using a split page to take notes and create questions. *Practice > Unit 4 > Activity 2*

LISTENING 1   ## Gravity at Work

OBJECTIVE ▶   You are going to listen to a discussion in a physics class. As you listen, gather information and ideas about how the laws of science affect our lives.

PREVIEW THE LISTENING

A. PREVIEW Look at the picture above. Have you seen this item before? What might it be used for? Why do you think it was invented? Share your ideas with a partner.

B. VOCABULARY Read aloud these words from Listening 1. Check (✓) the ones you know. Use a dictionary to define any new or unknown words. Then discuss with a partner how the words will relate to the unit.

affordable *(adj.)* 🔑	**intention** *(n.)* 🔑 OPAL
alternative *(n.)* 🔑 OPAL	**inventor** *(n.)*
force *(n.)* 🔑 OPAL	**power** *(v.)* 🔑
function *(v.)* 🔑 OPAL	**stream** *(v.)*
gear *(n.)* 🔑	**summarize** *(v.)* 🔑 OPAL
hazardous *(adj.)*	**throughout** *(prep.)* 🔑 OPAL

🔑 Oxford 5000™ words   OPAL Oxford Phrasal Academic Lexicon

iQ PRACTICE   Go online to listen and practice your pronunciation.
Practice ▸ Unit 4 ▸ Activity 3

WORK WITH THE LISTENING

🔊 **A. LISTEN AND TAKE NOTES** Listen to the discussion. Complete the notes in the right column of the chart.

iQ RESOURCES Go online to download extra vocabulary support.
Resources > Extra Vocabulary > Unit 4

Questions	Notes
	GravityLight
	_____ Reeves and Riddiford
	wanted to find _____
	works by _____
	gear inside GL _____
	Mr. Trash Wheel
	Baltimore has had a problem with
	_____
	invented by Kellett—_____
	description: _____
	how it works: _____

B. COMPOSE Read your notes and in the left column write questions about what you heard.

C. IDENTIFY Read the questions. Then listen again. Circle the correct answers.

1. Why does a pencil move toward the ground when you drop it?

    a. Because gravity attracts the smaller object to the bigger object

    b. Because a pencil is heavier than the air around it

2. Where are kerosene lights commonly used?

    a. In England

    b. In the developing world

3. Why did Reeves and Riddiford want to invent a light without a battery?

    a. Batteries contain dangerous chemicals.

    b. Batteries are expensive.

4. How many minutes of light does the GravityLight provide?

    a. 12 minutes

    b. 20 minutes

5. What caused Kellett to invent Mr. Trash Wheel?

    a. He was tired of his workplace being disgusting.

    b. He wanted a partnership with Baltimore City.

6. How much garbage has Mr. Trash Wheel kept out of the harbor?

    a. About a million pounds

    b. More than a million pounds

kerosene lamp

D. CATEGORIZE Read the statements. Write *T* (true) or *F* (false). Then correct each false statement to make it true.

____ 1. Kerosene lights are dirty, dangerous, and expensive.

____ 2. GravityLight is a light attached to a weight that slowly falls and powers the light.

____ 3. The parts for GravityLight are cheap, so it isn't an expensive product.

____ 4. Reeves and Riddiford think their light can help people throughout the world.

____ 5. Baltimore's trash comes from people throwing it in the street and from the wind blowing it out of garbage cans.

____ 6. Mr. Trash Wheel relies only on gravity to function.

____ 7. Mr. Trash Wheel collects trash in good and bad weather.

E. **EXTEND** Discuss the questions in a group.

1. What are some problems Reeves and Riddiford might face when they try to sell GravityLight?

2. Why do you think Kellett added the eyes to the top of Mr. Trash Wheel?

3. Would it surprise you to learn that Mr. Trash Wheel has become a tourist attraction in Baltimore? Why do you think that might be?

F. **VOCABULARY** Here are some words from Listening 1. Complete each sentence with the correct word.

affordable *(adj.)*	function *(v.)*	intention *(n.)*	stream *(v.)*
alternative *(n.)*	gear *(n.)*	inventor *(n.)*	summarize *(v.)*
force *(n.)*	hazardous *(adj.)*	power *(v.)*	throughout *(prep.)*

1. When you cry, tears _____ down your face.

2. The electric company makes enough energy to _____ the town.

3. Don't tell me the whole story. Just _____ it.

4. That jacket is too expensive. I need to find one that is more

   _____.

5. I can't ride my bicycle because the _____ is broken.

6. The _____ of the moving water pushes the wheel around.

7. I like to think about every _____ before I make a decision.

8. It's illegal to dump _____ chemicals in rivers and lakes.

9. Alexander Graham Bell was an important _____. When he made the first telephone, he changed history forever.

10. When designed well, a video game can _____ as an educational tool.

11. She is working with the _____ of saving money to pay for college.

12. There was art _____ the entire museum. Paintings, photographs, and sculptures were in every room.

waterwheel

iQ PRACTICE Go online for more practice with the vocabulary.
Practice > Unit 4 > Activity 4

iQ PRACTICE Go online for additional listening and comprehension.
Practice > Unit 4 > Activity 5

 # SAY WHAT YOU THINK

DISCUSS Work in a group to discuss the questions.

1. If you could choose which product to invest in, would you choose GravityLight or Mr. Trash Wheel? Why?

2. What other products do you know about like GravityLight that inventors have created from simple parts to help people in developing areas?

3. Would Mr. Trash Wheel be welcome in your city? Why or why not?

LISTENING SKILL Making inferences

We often understand ideas that the speaker has not actually stated. **Making inferences** involves "reading between the lines," or figuring out more than is actually said to understand the full meaning. Listen carefully to make inferences based on the information available to you.

In the excerpt below, the speaker, Rowan, tells us about the invention of Mr. Trash Wheel.

> So, this guy, John Kellett, is a sailor and an engineer in Baltimore. He worked for years in the harbor. He was tired of seeing all the garbage in the water, so he worked with the Waterfront Partnership of Baltimore to build a trash wheel.

Based on this information, we can infer that Mr. Trash Wheel was John Kellett's idea and that the Waterfront Partnership of Baltimore helped him to build it.

Often, speakers communicate how they feel about the ideas they are presenting. To fully understand someone, listen closely to infer attitudes and emotions. Pay attention to the following.

Speed and pitch: If a speaker is talking quickly, and his or her pitch goes up and down, this may indicate that the speaker is excited or passionate about the topic.

Tone: Does the speaker laugh or sound serious?

Descriptive words: Listen for words that express feelings and opinions, like *love, hate, terrible, wonderful, terrific,* and so on.

A. EVALUATE Listen to excerpts from Listening 1. Based on the statements in each excerpt, what can you infer? Circle the correct answers.

TIP FOR SUCCESS

Many tests require students to answer several inference questions. Learning to make inferences based on what you hear or read is an important part of preparing for tests.

Excerpt 1

a. The professor believes the students understand.

b. The professor isn't sure if the students understand.

Excerpt 2

a. The students were free to organize their presentations in the way that made sense to them.

b. The students should have organized their presentations in a particular way.

ACADEMIC LANGUAGE

Sometimes speakers will tell you which information they feel is the most important by using phrases like these to draw listeners' attention to specific points:
the most important
most importantly
is important to
a very important
one of the key
one of the most

⎦ **OPAL**
Oxford Phrasal Academic Lexicon

Excerpt 3

a. Kerosene lights are cheap.

b. Kerosene lights are efficient.

B. IDENTIFY Listen to the excerpts from Listening 1. Circle the correct answers.

1. In Excerpt 1, you can infer that the speaker is ____.

   a. bored by the GravityLight

   b. excited about the GravityLight

2. Circle the clue(s) that helped you to make the inference in item 1.

   a. the speaker's speed and pitch

   b. the speaker's tone or laughter

   c. the speaker's descriptive words

3. In Excerpt 2, you can infer that the speaker is ____.

   a. excited about Mr. Trash Wheel

   b. disappointed that Mr. Trash Wheel has not collected more trash

4. Circle the clue(s) that helped you to make the inference in item 3.

   a. the speaker's speed and pitch

   b. the speaker's tone or laughter

   c. the speaker's descriptive words

iQ PRACTICE Go online for more practice listening to make inferences.
Practice ⟩ Unit 4 ⟩ Activity 6

LISTENING 2 Moore's Law

OBJECTIVE ▶

You are going to watch a video and then listen to a related lecture. As you listen, gather information and ideas about how the laws of science affect our lives.

PREVIEW THE LISTENING

A. PREVIEW Moore's law predicted the small, fast technology that has resulted in the smartphones of today. If you were buying a new smartphone, what things would you consider? Look at the list. Check (✓) the things that are important to you.

☐ price　　　☐ screen size　　　☐ memory storage　　　☐ brand

☐ size　　　☐ speed　　　☐ battery life　　　☐ color

B. VOCABULARY Read aloud these words from Listening 2. Check (✓) the ones you know. Use a dictionary to define any new or unknown words. Then discuss with a partner how the words will relate to the unit.

astonishing *(adj.)* 🍌	**extent** *(n.)* 🍌 OPAL	**reflect** *(v.)* 🍌 OPAL
capacity *(n.)* 🍌 OPAL	**hilarious** *(adj.)* 🍌	**sophisticated** *(adj.)* 🍌
double *(v.)* 🍌	**noticeable** *(adj.)*	**target** *(n.)* 🍌 OPAL
dramatically *(adv.)* 🍌	**rapidly** *(adv.)* 🍌 OPAL	

🍌 Oxford 5000™ words　　　　　　　　　　OPAL Oxford Phrasal Academic Lexicon

iQ PRACTICE Go online to listen and practice your pronunciation.
Practice ⟩ Unit 4 ⟩ Activity 7

WORK WITH THE LISTENING

iQ RESOURCES Go online to watch the video.
Resources > *Video* > *Unit 4* > *Listening 2*

A. LISTEN AND TAKE NOTES Watch the video.* Then listen to the lecture. Take notes in the right section of the chart.

iQ RESOURCES Go online to download extra vocabulary support.
Resources > *Extra Vocabulary* > *Unit 4*

Questions	Notes on main ideas and important details

B. COMPOSE Read your notes and write questions about what you heard on the left.

C. CATEGORIZE Read the statements. Write *T* (true) or *F* (false). Then correct each false statement to make it true.

_____ 1. Moore said the number of transistors that could fit on a circuit board would double every two years.

_____ 2. The increase in transistors has doubled the price of computers.

_____ 3. Experts do not believe we are approaching the end of Moore's law.

_____ 4. MIT is working on a pill that turns a computer into medicine.

D. IDENTIFY Listening 2 mentions several different kinds of technology. Read the list below. Then watch and listen again and check (✓) which items you hear the speakers talk about.

☐ ATM   ☐ e-reader   ☐ smartwatch

☐ cell phone   ☐ GPS   ☐ tablet

☐ computer   ☐ laptop   ☐ virtual reality

☐ digital camera   ☐ smartphone

*Audio version available. Resources > Audio > Unit 4

E. IDENTIFY Based on the listening, what might experts believe about Moore's law? Read the list and check (✓) the things that scientists might have said.

☐ 1. "Moore's law has had very little impact on the technology industry."

☐ 2. "The truth is that Moore's law has made amazing things possible."

☐ 3. "Cell phones would have been developed without the help of Moore's law. It might have just taken longer."

☐ 4. "Moore's law will last forever, making technology smaller and smaller in the future."

☐ 5. "The future of technology is really hard to predict because there is a clear limit to Moore's law."

☐ 6. "Moore's law has directly impacted the way we buy technology. We expect tech companies to introduce new, faster, smaller products every couple of years."

F. DISCUSS Share your answers with a partner. Discuss why you selected the answers you checked.

G. DISCUSS Work in a group to discuss the questions.

1. How has shrinking technology affected society? If computers were still the size of a room, how would life be different?

2. How might the computer pill that is being developed by MIT benefit people? Would you agree to try it? Why or why not?

In Unit 3, you learned about checking the definitions of similar words to determine which word is appropriate in a context. Can you think of words that have meanings similar to *hilarious, rapidly,* or *sophisticated*? Look up those words in a dictionary and notice how their meanings are slightly different from the words in this list.

H. VOCABULARY Here are some words from Listening 2. Read the sentences. Then write each bold word next to the correct definition.

1. Prices have increased **dramatically** in the past few years. Everything is much more expensive than before.

2. The joke was **hilarious**. I couldn't stop laughing.

3. Computers are more **sophisticated** than they were even ten years ago. Technology has become very complex.

4. The change was really **noticeable** because it was so extreme.

5. **Double** all the ingredients in the recipe if you want to make the cake for twice as many people.

6. It's hard to understand the **extent** of the flood damage unless you see it from above in a helicopter.

7. It is **astonishing** how fast he can run. I just can't believe my eyes!

8. Cybersecurity is a **rapidly** growing industry. It seems as though new companies are opening every day.

9. The new policy **reflects** the company's new direction. It really shows what their values are.

10. The company set a **target** of making one million dollars in profit. They worked hard to meet it.

11. He has the **capacity** to get good grades, but he doesn't study very hard.

a. _____ (*adj.*) very funny

b. _____ (*v.*) to become or make something become twice as much or as many

c. _____ (*adj.*) easy to see or notice

d. _____ (*adj.*) very quickly

e. _____ (*adj.*) clever and complicated in the way that it works or is presented

f. _____ (*v.*) to show the nature of something or of someone's attitude or feeling

g. _____ (*adj.*) very surprising; difficult to believe

h. _____ (*n.*) how large, important, serious, etc., something is

i. _____ (*adv.*) very suddenly and to a very great and often surprising degree

j. _____ (n.) a result that you try to achieve

k. _____ (n.) the ability to understand or to do something

iQ PRACTICE Go online for more practice with the vocabulary.
Practice > Unit 4 > Activity 8

SAY WHAT YOU THINK

SYNTHESIZE Think about Listening 1 and Listening 2 as you discuss the questions.

1. How are Sir Isaac Newton and Gordon Moore similar, even though they lived 300 years apart?

2. The laws of science are based on observations about how nature works. Both listening texts show how this scientific knowledge can be used to change the world. What are other examples of science leading to important change?

VOCABULARY SKILL Word forms

Many words have several forms. For instance, a verb may have a noun form, an adjective form, and an adverb form. Notice all the forms of the verb *appreciate*.

> **Verb:** I **appreciate** all the help you have given us.
>
> **Noun:** We applauded to show our **appreciation**.
>
> **Adjective:** It feels great to lecture to an **appreciative** audience.
>
> **Adverb:** The children responded **appreciatively** when they received the gifts.

In some cases, different parts of speech of a word have the same form.

> **Noun:** John knew that he would never forget that **encounter** with the boss.
>
> **Verb:** When we arrive, I expect to **encounter** some problems.

When you look up a word in the dictionary, note its forms. This will help you build your vocabulary. Each word form will be marked with its part of speech. Common abbreviations for *verb, noun, adjective,* and *adverb* are *v., n., adj.,* and *adv*.

A. IDENTIFY Look at the verbs in bold. Circle the word on each line that is not a form of the bold verb. Use a dictionary to help you.

1. **produce** *(v.)*:   productive   prodigy   productivity

2. **consider** *(v.)*:   consideration   considerate   consistent

3. **develop** *(v.)*:   deviate   development   developer

4. **operate** *(v.)*:   orate   operation   operator

5. **reflect** *(v.)*:   reflection   reflex   reflective

6. **alternate** *(v.)*:   alternative   alternatively   altered

B. APPLY Complete the sentences with the correct form of the word in parentheses. Use a dictionary to help you.

1. You might wonder how a law of science is different from a

   _____ theory. (science, *adj.*)

2. _____, a law is something someone has observed about the

   world. (basic, *adv.*)

3. A law is always _____ and simple. (truth, *adj.*)

4. But, a theory is an _____ of why something happens.

   (explain, *n.*)

5. So, when Sir Isaac Newton observed the apple falling and _____

   gravity, he was making a law. (description, *v.*)

6. But, scientists didn't really understand how gravity worked until Einstein

   _____ his theory of relativity. (development, *v.*)

iQ PRACTICE   Go online for more practice using word forms.
Practice > Unit 4 > Activity 9

CRITICAL THINKING STRATEGY

Distinguishing between similar words

When you distinguish between things, you show you understand how things are different. This is a helpful skill to understand why a speaker chooses one word instead of another. For instance, if someone says a joke is funny, he or she probably smiled or laughed a little. However, if someone says a joke is hilarious, he or she probably laughed loudly and for a long time. Both *funny* and *hilarious* have the same basic meaning, but knowing the difference can help you understand more about the speaker's message.

iQ PRACTICE   Go online to watch the Critical Thinking Video and check your comprehension. *Practice > Unit 4 > Activity 10*

C. IDENTIFY Read the sentences and match them with the correct message.

_____ 1. I was **afraid**.   a. It was a little scary, but I am fine.

_____ 2. I was **terrified**.   b. It was so scary that I am still shaking.

_____ 3. The car was **cheap**.   a. It was a good price. I can pay for it.

_____ 4. The car was **affordable**.   b. The car was so inexpensive that I'm
                                              worried it will break down.

_____ 5. I caught a **disease** on my trip.   a. I got seriously sick on vacation.

_____ 6. I caught a **bug** on my trip.   b. I got a little sick on vacation.

SPEAKING

OBJECTIVE ▶

At the end of this unit, you are going to create a role-play about presenting a business plan for a new product. During the presentation, you will need to be able to politely avoid answering questions.

GRAMMAR Present perfect and present perfect continuous

Present Perfect

The **present perfect** can describe actions that happened at an unspecified time in the past. The present perfect construction is *has/have* + past participle.

> He **has worked** with the Waterfront Partnership of Baltimore to build a trash wheel.
> (They finished the trash wheel in the past, but we don't know exactly when.)

The present perfect also describes actions that started in the past and continue in the present time. The words *for* and *since* are used to describe actions that started at a definite time in the past.

> This city **has had** a problem with garbage in its harbor for many years.
> (The city started having the problem many years ago, and it still has the problem.)
> It's already **taken** more than a million pounds of trash out of the water.
> (It started taking trash out of the water when it was built, and it is still taking trash out of the water.)

The present perfect is often used to talk about past actions that happened more than once in the past.

> It **has** already **been** sold in countries like Kenya.
> (The company sold it multiple times in the recent past.)

Present Perfect Continuous

The **present perfect continuous** describes actions that started in the past but were not finished. By choosing the present perfect continuous, you are emphasizing that the action is continuing. The present perfect continuous construction is *has/have* + *been* + present participle.

> Many people around the world **have been using** kerosene lights.
> (They started using them in the past, and they are still using them.)
> John Kellett **has been working** for years in the harbor.
> (He started working in the harbor many years ago. He still works there.)

iQ RESOURCES Go online to watch the Grammar Skill Video.
Resources > Video > Unit 4 > Grammar Skill Video

A. APPLY Rewrite the sentences. Use the present perfect.

1. Alonzo started the project.

    Alonzo has started the project.

2. I thought a lot about this project over the past few years.

    _____

3. Ellen took several physics classes at the university.

    _____

4. Min-ju gave a sample of the product to her friends to test.

    _____

5. The company won three awards over the past year, and it will probably win more.

    _____

TIP FOR SUCCESS

When using present perfect and present perfect continuous verbs, speakers often contract *have* and *has* so they sound like *'ve* and *'s*. Listen for these contractions to help you understand a speaker's meaning.

B. IDENTIFY Complete the conversation. Circle the correct verb form. Then practice the conversation with a partner.

solar windows

Jamal: Hey, Ryan! Guess what? Rashida and I (have started / have been starting) a new company recently. It's called Solectric.
1

Ryan: Oh, wow! That's great! What does your company do?

Jamal: Well, over the past couple of years, we (have worked / have been working) on technology that focuses the sun so we can catch and keep the energy. We want to sell the technology to solar energy companies.
2

Ryan: Wait, what? How (have you come / have you been coming) up with that?
3

Jamal: So, according to the first law of thermodynamics, energy can't be created or destroyed. It can only be changed. So we (have found / have been finding) a
4
way to use a special paint over normal window glass to catch the energy from the sun, make it stronger, save it, and change it into electricity.

Ryan: That's amazing! How much of the paint
(have you sold / have you been selling) so far?
5

Jamal: We (have worked / have been working) on the product for years but just
6
developed the sales presentation last week.

Ryan: That's great news, Jamal!

iQ PRACTICE Go online for more practice with the present perfect and present perfect continuous. *Practice > Unit 4 > Activity 11*

iQ PRACTICE Go online for the Grammar Expansion: future forms: *will, be going to,* and future continuous. *Practice > Unit 4 > Activity 12*

PRONUNCIATION Basic intonation patterns

Intonation Pattern

When you are speaking, the pitch of your voice goes up and down. This change in pitch is called an **inonation pattern**. Intonation patterns carry a lot of information. For instance, your intonation will let your listener know if you are asking a question or making a statement. It's important to use the correct intonation pattern to effectively communicate your meaning.

Rising/Falling

One of the most common intonation patterns in English is the *rising/falling* pattern, where the pitch rises before the last word and falls on the last word. This pattern is common in simple declarative sentences, direct commands, and *wh-* questions.

I enjoyed it very much.

Hand me that brush, please.

What have you seen?

Rising

For *yes/no* questions, use a rising intonation pattern.

Are you concerned?

A. ANALYZE Listen to each sentence. Write *R* (rising intonation pattern) or *RF* (rising/falling pattern). Then repeat each sentence.

_____ 1. Gordon Moore made an important prediction.

_____ 2. Where did he work?

_____ 3. Did Moore's law create new industries?

_____ 4. What has Moore's law changed?

_____ 5. Will Moore's law continue forever?

_____ 6. Computers are not rare and expensive anymore.

_____ 7. Can you imagine a day without your smartphone?

_____ 8. How do you feel about computers being able to read your mind?

B. APPLY Listen to the conversation. Draw arrows to show the intonation patterns. Listen again and repeat. Then practice the conversation with a partner.

Alex: What's that?

Lee: It's a cool new flashlight.

Alex: What's so cool about it?

Lee: The power for it comes from the heat of my hand.

Alex: How does that work?

Lee: It's the thermoelectric effect. It changes the heat into electricity.

Alex: Can I see it?

Lee: Here you are.

Alex: It really works!

iQ PRACTICE   Go online for more practice with basic intonation patterns.
Practice > Unit 4 > Activity 13

There are times when you prefer not to answer a question that someone has asked you. Here are several ways that you can avoid answering questions without being impolite.

Refuse politely.

A: Who did you vote for?

B: Actually, I'd prefer not to say.

A: How have your sales been so far this year?

B: Sorry, but we're not ready to release that information.

Ask another question.

A: What do you think of the new CEO?

B: What do you think?

Answer a different question.

You can provide related information without addressing the question that was actually asked.

A: Are you looking for a new job?

B: I like this job very much.

Use vague phrases.

Phrases like *you might say* or *one could conclude* avoid stating your own opinion directly.

A: What do you think about the new smartphone?

B: You might say it's a good product for some people.

Refusing politely is the simplest and most direct way to avoid answering a question. Using vague phrases is the least direct way. These strategies can be used in all types of situations.

A. CATEGORIZE Listen to the conversations. With a partner, discuss what strategy each speaker uses to avoid answering a question. Then practice the conversations with your partner.

1. A: How old are you?

   B: I'd rather not say.

2. A: What did you think of the company president's speech?

   B: You might say it gives a very unique point of view.

3. A: Hello. Is Nick there?

   B: Who's calling?

4. A: Is Joseph doing a good job?

   B: Joseph is a very hard worker.

5. A: Can I have your address, please?

   B: I'm sorry, but I don't give out that information.

6. A: Where were you on Friday?

   B: Why do you need to know?

B. COMPOSE Read the questions. Write responses that avoid answering the questions directly. Then practice with a partner.

1. A: Would you like to invest in our new company, Solectric?

   B: _____

2. A: What do you think of the new heat-powered flashlight?

   B: _____

3. A: Would you like information on our latest products?

   B: _____

4. A: What is your email address?

   B: _____

iQ PRACTICE Go online for more practice avoiding answering questions.
Practice > Unit 4 > Activity 14

UNIT ASSIGNMENT

OBJECTIVE ▶

Present a business plan

In this assignment, you are going to create a role-play about presenting a business plan for a new product. Your classmates will be potential investors in your business. As you prepare your presentation, think about the Unit Question, "How do the laws of science affect our lives?" Use information from Listening 1, Listening 2, and your work in this unit to support your presentation. Refer to the Self-Assessment checklist on page 100.

CONSIDER THE IDEAS

What kinds of science-based products would you be interested in making or selling? Consider the products you have heard about in this unit, the information below, and any other products related to the laws of science you can think of. Discuss these questions in a group.

1. What kinds of products do you think would sell well? Why? Who would buy them?

2. Would you be willing to invest money to support someone's business that was making the following products? Why or why not?

a. **Vibeat:** Headphones that convert sound into vibration so the deaf can experience music (law of reflection)

b. **Fly-bot:** Tiny drone that processes what it "sees" very rapidly, allowing it to move quickly in dangerous situations (Moore's law)

c. **Synthetic jet propulsion system:** Lighter pieces of a rocket that reduce the amount of fuel a rocket needs to take off (Newton's third law of motion)

d. **Floating trash collector:** Tubes in the ocean that collect garbage and don't hurt fish (Archimedes's buoyancy principle)

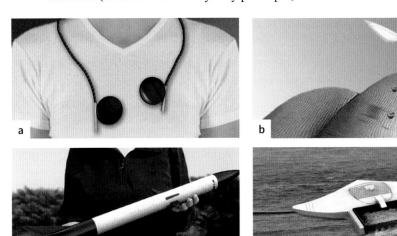

a

b

c

d

PREPARE AND SPEAK

A. GATHER IDEAS Read the list of questions an investor might ask an entrepreneur before lending him or her money to start a new business. Add questions based on your discussion in the Consider the Ideas activity.

You and the product

1. What makes the product that you are selling unique?

2. How much experience do you have running a business?

3. _____

The market

4. Who will you sell your product to? That is, who is your target market?

5. Who else sells products like yours? That is, who is your competition?

6. _____

The deal

7. How much does it cost to make the product, and how much will you sell it for?

8. How much money do you want from an investor to help start your business?

9. _____

B. ORGANIZE IDEAS Choose a science-based product for which you would like to develop a business plan and get investors.

1. Prepare responses to the questions in Activity A. Are there any questions in the list you might want to avoid answering? How will you avoid answering them?

2. Think about your presentation. How will you make it interesting for potential investors (the class) and capture their attention?

C. SPEAK Follow these steps. Refer to the Self-Assessment checklist below before you begin.

1. Present your business plan for a science-based product to potential investors (the class).

2. Answer any questions they might have, and ask them any questions you have.

iQ PRACTICE Go online for your alternate Unit Assignment.
Practice > Unit 4 > Activity 15

CHECK AND REFLECT

A. CHECK Think about the Unit Assignment as you complete the Self-Assessment checklist.

SELF-ASSESSMENT	Yes	No
I was able to speak easily about the topic.	☐	☐
My partner, group, and class understood me.	☐	☐
I used the present perfect and the present perfect continuous.	☐	☐
I used vocabulary from the unit.	☐	☐
I used strategies to avoid answering questions.	☐	☐
I used correct intonation patterns.	☐	☐

B. REFLECT Discuss these questions with a partner or group.

1. What is something new you learned in this unit?

2. Look back at the Unit Question—How do the laws of science affect our lives? Is your answer different now than it was when you started this unit? If yes, how is it different? Why?

iQ PRACTICE Go to the online discussion board to discuss the questions.
Practice > Unit 4 > Activity 16

TRACK YOUR SUCCESS

iQ PRACTICE Go online to check the words and phrases you have learned in
this unit. *Practice > Unit 4 > Activity 17*

Check (✓) the skills and strategies you learned. If you need more work on a
skill, refer to the page(s) in parentheses.

NOTE-TAKING	☐ I can use a split page to take notes and create questions. (p. 80)
LISTENING	☐ I can make inferences. (p. 85)
VOCABULARY	☐ I can use word forms. (p. 91)
CRITICAL THINKING	☐ I can distinguish between similar words. (p. 92)
GRAMMAR	☐ I can use the present perfect and the present perfect continuous. (p. 93)
PRONUNCIATION	☐ I can use basic intonation patterns. (p. 95)
SPEAKING	☐ I can avoid answering questions. (p. 97)

OBJECTIVE ▶   ☐ I can gather information and ideas to create a role-play about presenting a
business plan for a new product.

5

Nutritional Science

NOTE-TAKING	editing notes after a lecture
LISTENING	understanding bias in a presentation
CRITICAL THINKING	evaluating information
VOCABULARY	prefixes and suffixes
GRAMMAR	comparative forms of adjectives and adverbs
PRONUNCIATION	common intonation patterns
SPEAKING	expressing interest during a conversation

How has science changed the food we eat?

A. Discuss these questions with your classmates.

1. Which is most important in the food you choose: flavor, cost, or nutrition? Why?

2. How does TV advertising affect what food you eat?

3. Look at the photo. What is the person doing? Would you eat food grown in this field? Why or why not?

B. Listen to *The Q Classroom* online. Then answer these questions.

1. Yuna says packaged food is good for us because it has more vitamins and less fat. Felix and Marcus state that packaged food is not healthy. Who do you agree with? Why?

2. Sophy says that because of science, we can grow bigger plants and animals. What might be an advantage to having bigger food?

iQ PRACTICE Go to the online discussion board to discuss the Unit Question with your classmates. *Practice > Unit 5 > Activity 1*

UNIT OBJECTIVE

Watch a video and listen to a radio report and gather information and ideas to participate in a debate on food science.

In order to remember most of what you hear, it is a good idea to review your notes within 24 hours after a lecture. As you read your notes, annotate them (add notes to a text, giving explanations or comments):

1. Underline or highlight key ideas.

2. Cross out information that isn't important.

3. Use the extra space on the paper to add your thoughts and make connections between the lecture and the information in your textbook.

4. Use a dictionary to look up all new key words. Write the definition or translation.

5. Make notes about what you don't understand so you can ask your teacher later.

6. Add a short summary of your notes.

A. APPLY Listen to the lecture about food as medicine. Then edit the notes based on the first four annotation tips above. Compare your edits with a partner.

Peking duck

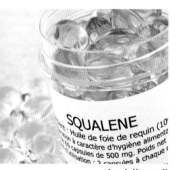
shark liver oil

Using food in place of medicine

1. China—Peking duck

    a. Famous and delicious

    b. Red rice powder on duck skin

    c. Lowers cholesterol (?)

    d. Fewer Chinese people get heart disease than other countries

2. Brazil—Hammerhead shark liver oil

    a. Indigenous (native) populations off the coast of Brazil

    b. Cure asthma (trouble breathing)

    c. Endangered (?)

    d. Now, researchers are testing asthma drugs made from oil from nurse & blue sharks

B. COMPOSE Review the notes again. Write two follow-up questions and a short summary based on the fifth and sixth annotation tips above. Share your summary with a partner.

iQ PRACTICE Go online for more practice editing notes after a lecture. *Practice > Unit 5 > Activity 2*

LISTENING 1

OBJECTIVE ▶

Improving Farming with Flying Robots

You are going to watch a video news report about how technology can help farmers. As you watch, gather information and ideas about how the use of drones, or flying robots, might change the food we eat.

PREVIEW THE LISTENING

A. PREVIEW Discuss the questions in a small group.

1. Farming can be a difficult job. What problems do you think farmers might face today?

2. How do you think technology like drones might help farmers? What can drones do to make farming easier and more efficient?

B. VOCABULARY Read aloud these words from Listening 1. Check (✓) the ones you know. Use a dictionary to define any new or unknown words. Then discuss with a partner how the words will relate to the unit.

buzz *(v.)*	**infection** *(n.)* 🔑	**revolution** *(n.)* 🔑
distribute *(v.)* 🔑 OPAL	**load** *(n.)* 🔑	**suffer** *(v.)* 🔑
dominate *(v.)* 🔑 OPAL	**precision** *(n.)* 🔑 OPAL	**survey** *(n.)* 🔑 OPAL
ignorance *(n.)* 🔑	**productivity** *(n.)* 🔑	

🔑 Oxford 5000™ words   OPAL Oxford Phrasal Academic Lexicon

iQ PRACTICE Go online to listen and practice your pronunciation.
Practice ▸ Unit 5 ▸ Activity 3

WORK WITH THE LISTENING

iQ RESOURCES Go online to watch the video.
Resources > Video > Unit 5 > Listening 1

A. LISTEN AND TAKE NOTES Watch the video.* Read the student's notes about how farmers can use drones. Match the note headings with the correct rows.

iQ RESOURCES Go online to download extra vocabulary support.
Resources > Extra Vocabulary > Unit 5

Concerns about using robots	Possible uses for drones	Pressures on farmers
	too hard to use not reliable enough too expensive we think of drones as military weapons	
	feed more people lower the chemical load use less water farms are bigger than before fewer workers on the farms crops can get disease/infections	
	get data measure their farms look for disease they can see if chemicals should be sprayed on the crops	

B. IDENTIFY Edit the notes. Underline or highlight key words and phrases and cross out words that are not important. Also, explain or define new vocabulary and make notes about what you still don't understand.

C. DISCUSS Work with a partner. Use your notes to summarize the information in the video. Answer the questions.

1. Why are people concerned about using robots?

2. What pressures do farmers face today?

3. How could farmers use drones?

* Audio version available. *Resources > Audio > Unit 5*

D. IDENTIFY Watch the video again. Check (✓) the main ideas mentioned in the report.

☐ 1. Drones are the future of aviation.

☐ 2. Drones can help farmers feed more people.

☐ 3. Farms are getting bigger and bigger.

☐ 4. Farmers can use drones to get big data on their crops.

☐ 5. Farmers have to spray their crops to fight disease.

☐ 6. Cows are milked by milking machines nowadays.

☐ 7. Farming is the biggest industry in the world.

☐ 8. Drones are not weapons.

E. INTERPRET Read the comments below. Do you think the farmers would be more likely to use drone technology on their farms or less likely? Write *ML* (more likely) or *LL* (less likely).

____ 1. "I have a real problem getting to all the parts of my farm. It's huge, and I don't have time to drive around it as often as I should."

____ 2. "I'm not sure using a drone is safe. What happens to the data it records? Would other farmers be able to get information about my crops?"

____ 3. "We bought our farm as a change from city living. We produce small batches of high-quality goat cheese. Our goats are like family members."

____ 4. "I love how technology makes farming easier. I have a GPS-guided planting system and sensors that tell us where to water."

____ 5. "Drones are expensive, and changes in the weather have caused our crops to fail the past two years. We don't have extra money for technology."

____ 6. "I need a way to reduce the amount of chemicals I use to keep my crops healthy. I often overspray because I can't get good data on my plants."

F. VOCABULARY Here are some words from Listening 1. Read the sentences. Then write each bold word next to the correct definition.

1. I hate to admit my **ignorance**, but I don't know anything about this topic.

2. The money was **distributed** evenly to each person who won.

3. You can put your **load** of laundry in the washing machine.

4. She **dominated** the conversation by talking a lot and not letting anyone else speak.

5. It is important that surgeons operate with **precision**. If they are not careful, they might hurt their patients.

6. The social media **revolution** changed the way we interact with our friends.

7. I **suffer** from leg pains at night, so I am going to talk to my doctor.

8. He read a **survey** of the country's history to increase his general knowledge about it.

9. Can you please turn off your phone so it doesn't **buzz** in the meeting?

10. He looked at the trees to find any sign of **infection** that would show the trees were sick.

11. How much you are paid depends on your **productivity**.

a. _____ (*n.*) the quality of being exact, accurate, and careful

b. _____ (*n.*) the total amount that something can carry or contain

c. _____ (*n.*) a great change in conditions, ways of working, beliefs, etc., that affects large numbers of people

d. _____ (*v.*) to make a sound like a bee

e. _____ (*v.*) to control or have a lot of influence over somebody/ something

f. _____ (*n.*) the rate at which a worker, a company, or a country produces goods

g. _____ (*n.*) a lack of knowledge or information about something

h. _____ (*n.*) an illness that is caused by bacteria or a virus

i. _____ (*v.*) to be badly affected by a disease, pain, sadness, a lack of something, etc.

j. _____ (*v.*) to share between a number of people

k. _____ (*n.*) a general study, view, or description of something

iQ PRACTICE Go online for more practice with the vocabulary.
Practice > Unit 5 > Activity 4

iQ PRACTICE Go online for additional listening and comprehension.
Practice > Unit 5 > Activity 5

? SAY WHAT YOU THINK

DISCUSS Work in a group to discuss the questions.

1. The scientist in the report says that his job "is to make [drones] cheap and easy and ubiquitous, and then ultimately the users figure out what the application is for." What do you think this means? Do you agree or disagree that this is a good way to do things? Why?

2. Do you think using drones on farms is a good idea? Why?

LISTENING SKILL   Understanding bias in a presentation

Bias is a strong feeling for or against something. Understanding the bias in a presentation is important. Speakers may express biases even when they're trying to sound objective. In Listening 1, the speaker mentions some problems with using drones on farms, but the speaker's bias appears to be in favor of technology and farming.

There are several clues to help you understand the bias of a presentation.

Title: Listening 1 is called "Improving Farming with Flying Robots." This is a positive idea, and it sounds very definite. This probably means the video is in favor of using drones in farming. A different title, such as "Some Farmers Believe That Drones May Increase Food Production," does not show such a strong bias.

Introduction: Pay attention to how a speaker introduces a topic. For example, if a speaker starts with, *I'm going to talk about all the benefits to using technology on farms*, that statement alone tells you the speaker's bias.

Imbalance: Presentations with a bias usually report on both sides of the issue, but the information is not balanced well. In Listening 1, most of the video is about how drones can help farmers, and only a small part of the video is about the possible problems of using drones.

Information source: Consider who is providing the information. For example, suppose a company that manufactures drones paid for this report. Knowing that the company makes drones can help you decide how much to trust the information.

 A. IDENTIFY Listen to the short report. Then answer the questions.

1. Check (✓) the clues you hear that tell you the bias.

   ☐ Title

   ☐ Introduction

   ☐ Imbalance

   ☐ Information source

2. Is the speaker against or in favor of organic food?

B. IDENTIFY Listen to excerpts from four news reports. What bias is being shown in each report? Circle the correct answers.

Excerpt 1

a. Some scientists believe there are many causes of obesity.

b. Some scientists believe fast food is a main cause of obesity.

Excerpt 2

a. Drinking soda may cause heart disease.

b. Drinking soda is part of a healthy lifestyle.

Excerpt 3

a. Drinking too much tea can be harmful.

b. Drinking tea is an old tradition.

Excerpt 4

a. Food labels can help us make good choices.

b. Food labels can be difficult to believe.

iQ PRACTICE Go online for more practice listening to understand bias in a presentation. *Practice > Unit 5 > Activity 6*

LISTENING 2   The Science Behind Food Cravings

OBJECTIVE ▶

You are going to listen to a radio report about food cravings. A *food craving* is a strong desire to eat a specific food. Scientists disagree about why people get these food cravings. As you listen to the report, gather information and ideas about how science affects the food we eat.

PREVIEW THE LISTENING

A. PREVIEW What kinds of food do you crave? Do you usually give in to your craving and eat the food or not? Discuss with a partner.

B. VOCABULARY Read aloud these words from Listening 2. Check (✓) the ones you know. Use a dictionary to define any new or unknown words. Then discuss with a partner how the words will relate to the unit.

alter *(v.)* ♪ OPAL	disturbing *(adj.)* ♪	reaction *(n.)* ♪ OPAL
compound *(v.)*	ethics *(n.)* ♪ OPAL	ultimate *(adj.)* ♪ OPAL
consumer *(n.)* ♪	intense *(adj.)* ♪	
debate *(n.)* ♪ OPAL	modification *(n.)* ♪	

♪ Oxford 5000™ words   OPAL Oxford Phrasal Academic Lexicon

iQ PRACTICE Go online to listen and practice your pronunciation.
Practice › Unit 5 › Activity 7

WORK WITH THE LISTENING

A. LISTEN AND TAKE NOTES Listen to the radio report. Complete the notes on the speakers and their comments.

Speaker	Job	Comments
Lara Jones	nutritionist	• food cravings affect _____ • might be message from body signaling _____ _____ chips craving = _____ chocolate craving = _____
Dr. Svacina	dietary psychologist	• disagrees → we don't crave all foods high in magnesium (e.g., _____, _____) • cravings can come from _____ • _____ also affects cravings Americans → _____ Egyptians → _____
Howazen Al Ganem	professor of ethics in advertising	• TV images of _____ cause cravings • need to think about ethics of _____ _____ • adults can change _____

B. DISCUSS Compare your notes with a partner. Whose comments and opinions do you think are more likely to be true? Why? Have any of the speakers changed the way you think about food cravings?

C. IDENTIFY Listen to the radio report again. Circle the correct answers.

1. In general, the panel of experts on the radio show agree that

   _____.

   a. the problem of food cravings affects most people

   b. the cause of food cravings is clear

   c. food cravings are biological

2. According to the radio report, _____.

   a. people should eat more junk food

   b. food cravings are never the result of a need for a nutrient

   c. food cravings may be caused by certain feelings

3. According to the report, TV viewers should probably _____.

   a. stop watching TV with their children

   b. walk away when the food advertisements come on

   c. change the laws to end food advertising

4. In general, the speakers _____ of food cravings.

   a. completely explained the causes

   b. didn't explain any of the causes

   c. explained some possible causes

D. CATEGORIZE Read the statements. Write *T* (true) or *F* (false). Then correct each false statement to make it true.

____ 1. Food cravings usually appear quickly and without warning.

____ 2. According to some nutritionists, a food craving is caused by having too much of a particular nutrient.

____ 3. Some scientists believe that food cravings come from positive emotions.

____ 4. Sometimes we only crave a kind of food because we see it around us or on TV.

____ 5. Eating a little bit of the food we crave can make the craving disappear.

E. EVALUATE Read the comments below. Which of the speakers from the radio report would be most likely to say them? Match the speaker with the comment.

____ 1. The radio show host

____ 2. Dr. Svacina, a dietary psychologist

____ 3. Lara Jones, a nutritionist

____ 4. Howazen Al Ganem, a professor of ethics in advertising

a. "A person who craves cheese may need more omega-3 fatty acids in their body. Instead of eating cheese, the person could eat walnuts or salmon. These are healthier choices and contain high levels of this nutrient."

b. "Recent research has shown us that children see a lot of TV advertisements for fast food. One study found that American preschoolers saw 2.8 fast-food ads on TV every day in 2012. That means children may be experiencing junk food cravings now more than ever before."

c. "Doing things to reduce the stress you have in your life might also reduce your food cravings. Try to do some yoga, take a walk, or call a friend. Feeling calmer may result in fewer trips to the refrigerator."

d. "I am glad to know that I am not alone in my food cravings. It appears that many other people have the same cravings. The key for me will be to limit myself to a healthy amount when I really feel like eating a whole bar or bag."

F. DISCUSS Work in a group to discuss the questions.

1. Advertisers use images of food to convince you to buy their product. Can you think of an advertisement you have seen that was very effective? What was the food, and why might the advertisement trigger a food craving?

2. Some experts suggest eating a little bit of the food you crave in order to stop the craving. Do you think this is good advice? Why or why not? What other things can people do to overcome food cravings?

VOCABULARY
SKILL REVIEW

In Unit 4, you learned about word forms. Try to find different word forms for the following vocabulary words in Activity G: *consumer, disturbing, ethics, modification, reaction.* Use a dictionary to help you.

G. VOCABULARY Here are some words from Listening 2. Complete each sentence with the correct word.

alter *(v.)*	debate *(n.)*	intense *(adj.)*	reaction *(n.)*
compound *(v.)*	disturbing *(adj.)*	modification *(n.)*	ultimate *(adj.)*
consumer *(n.)*	ethics *(n.)*		

1. I don't eat enough vegetables. To _____ the problem, my grocery store does not have much fresh produce.

2. I get _____ headaches. They are very strong.

3. I find it very _____ that people eat so much processed food. How can they eat that stuff instead of fruits and vegetables?

4. Advertisers try to catch the interest of any _____ who will want to buy their products.

5. When they said the newly created carrots were bright red, my first _____ was to say I didn't believe it.

6. We need to _____ our diet. I want to reduce the amount of processed food we eat.

7. Some people wanted the new factory in their town and some didn't. The _____ over building the new factory went on for years.

8. I think a bowl of ice cream with whipped cream is the _____ dessert. Nothing could be better than that!

9. I question the _____ of creating "superfoods." I'm not sure I agree that genetic engineering is always good.

10. This corn is very similar to normal corn, but scientists made a small _____ to its genes that makes it resist disease.

iQ PRACTICE Go online for more practice with the vocabulary.
Practice > Unit 5 > Activity 8

CRITICAL THINKING STRATEGY

Evaluating information

We can't believe everything we hear. **Evaluating information** is an important part of thinking critically. One step in evaluating information is identifying speaker bias, which you learned about in the Listening Skill. We need to think about who the speaker is and if he or she is a real expert on the subject. Another step is listening for the speaker to provide proof. We can also compare what we hear to our own experience.

iQ PRACTICE Go online to watch the Critical Thinking Video and check your comprehension. *Practice › Unit 5 › Activity 9*

H. EVALUATE Listen to the speakers. Complete the checklist evaluating the information each speaker shares.

	Speaker 1	Speaker 2	Speaker 3
The speaker is not biased.	☐	☐	☐
The speaker is an expert.	☐	☐	☐
The speaker provides proof.	☐	☐	☐
The speaker's ideas agree with my life experience.	☐	☐	☐

I. RESTATE Do you believe the speakers? Why or why not? Listen again. Complete the sentences with evidence in the speakers' words. Then share your opinions and reasons with a partner.

Speaker 1	I believe / don't believe the speaker because . . .
Speaker 2	I believe / don't believe the speaker because . . .
Speaker 3	I believe / don't believe the speaker because . . .

SAY WHAT YOU THINK

SYNTHESIZE Think about Listening 1 and Listening 2 as you discuss the questions.

1. Listening 1 described how farmers might use science to grow more food. Listening 2 is about how science can explain our eating habits. Which research were you most interested in? Which is more important for your life? For the world? Why?

2. Listening 1 was one expert's presentation. Listening 2 was a conversation among three experts. Do you prefer to get information from one source or from a conversation among several sources? How do you prefer to hear information?

VOCABULARY SKILL Prefixes and suffixes

Prefixes

Adding a **prefix** to the beginning of a word changes the meaning of the word. Understanding a prefix can help you identify the meaning of a word.

Prefix	Meaning	Example
dis-	opposite of	disorders
under-	less than enough	underdeveloped
re-	again	rebound
un-	not	uneasy

Suffixes

Adding a suffix to the end of a word often changes the part of speech. For example, adding *-ly* to the adjective *wide* changes the word to the adverb *widely*.

Suffix	Meaning	Example
-al, -ic	(*adj.*) about, connected with	chemical, genetic
-(at)ion	(*n.*) a state or process	reaction
-ist	(*n.*) a person who does	scientist
-less	(*adj.*) not having something	seedless
-(al)ly	(*adv.*) in a particular way	genetically
-ness	(*n.*) a quality	freshness

A. APPLY Write the meaning of each word. Look at the prefixes in the chart on page 116 to help you.

1. disapprove _____

2. redo _____

3. unfair _____

4. underfeed _____

5. untie _____

6. dislike _____

B. APPLY Look at the words and phrases below. Write the correct form of the word. Use the suffixes in the chart on page 116 to help you.

1. science (*n.* person) _scientist_   4. no weight (*adj.*) _____

2. origin (*adv.*) _____   5. about a topic (*adj.*) _____

3. unique (*n.* quality) _____   6. relate (*n.*) _____

C. COMPOSE Choose five words from Activities A and B. Write a sentence for each word. Then take turns reading your sentences to a partner.

iQ PRACTICE   Go online for more practice using prefixes and suffixes.
Practice > Unit 5 > Activity 10

SPEAKING

OBJECTIVE ▶

At the end of this unit, you are going to participate in a debate on food science, stating and supporting your opinions about food modification. During the debate, you will need to be able to use comparative forms of adjectives and adverbs and express interest in a conversation.

GRAMMAR Comparative forms of adjectives and adverbs

Comparative forms of adjectives and adverbs compare two things or actions. The rules for making comparatives are similar for both adjectives and adverbs.

Condition	Rule	Example
one-syllable adjectives	add -er	older
one-syllable adverbs		faster
one-syllable adjectives ending in -e	add -r	nicer
two-syllable adjectives ending in -y	change the y to i and add -er	healthier
most other adjectives	use more or less before the word	more interesting
all other adverbs		less naturally

Some adjectives take either -er or more.

narrow	→	narrower, more narrow
simple	→	simpler, more simple
quiet	→	quieter, more quiet
gentle	→	gentler, more gentle
handsome	→	handsomer, more handsome

Some adjectives and adverbs are irregular. This means the comparative adjective and adverb forms are not based on the base forms.

good	→	better	badly	→	worse
well	→	better	far	→	farther / further
bad	→	worse	little	→	less

To compare things or actions, use the word *than* after the comparative adjective or adverb.

Vegetables are healthier **than** junk food.

Many people are concerned about eating more healthfully **than** they were in the past.

iQ RESOURCES Go online to watch the Grammar Skill Video.
Resources › Video › Unit 5 › Grammar Skill Video

A. APPLY Write the comparative forms of the adjectives and adverbs. Then work with a partner. Take turns saying sentences using these comparative forms.

1. flavorful _____

2. uneasy _____

3. high _____

4. tasty _____

5. widely _____

6. unnatural _____

7. acceptable _____

8. bad _____

9. loyal _____

10. expensive _____

B. CREATE Work with a partner. Take turns asking and answering comparative questions.

Example: ice cream / delicious / chocolate / strawberry

A: *Which kind of ice cream do you think is more delicious, chocolate or strawberry?*

B: *I think strawberry ice cream is more delicious than chocolate ice cream.*

1. juice / sweet / pineapple / orange

2. peach / flavorful / preserved / fresh

3. TV show / disturbing / the news / reality TV

4. drink / widely enjoyed / tea / coffee

5. food / expensive / organic / genetically engineered

iQ PRACTICE Go online for more practice with comparative forms of adjectives and adverbs. *Practice > Unit 5 > Activity 11*

iQ PRACTICE Go online for the Grammar Expansion: *So . . . that* and *such a(n) . . . that. Practice > Unit 5 > Activity 12*

PRONUNCIATION Common intonation patterns

Intonation is an important part of communicating your ideas. There are common intonation patterns for specific conversational actions. Make sure you are using the correct pattern to help express your meaning.

To ask for clarification, use a rising intonation.

> This tomato is genetically altered?
>
> **Meaning:** I am not sure I heard you, or I am not sure I understand you.

To express surprise, use a rising intonation.

> You eat five sandwiches a day?
>
> **Meaning:** I am surprised by this information.

To list items, use a rising intonation for each item on the list. For the last item, use a rising/falling intonation.

> I ate eggs, toast, and cereal.
>
> **Meaning:** I ate these three things.

For *yes/no* questions, use a rising intonation.

> Would you like coffee?
>
> **Meaning:** You can say *yes* or *no* to my question.

To offer a choice between two things, use a rising/falling intonation.

> Would you like coffee or iced tea?
>
> **Meaning:** Which would you prefer?

 A. APPLY Listen to the sentences. Draw intonation arrows over each one. Then practice saying the sentences with a partner.

TIP FOR SUCCESS

When you listen to the radio, focus on the speakers' intonation. Pay attention to how they use their voices to express ideas and emotions.

1. What? You've never eaten a tomato?

2. Do you prefer water or juice?

3. My favorite foods are rice, yams, and pizza.

4. What did you say? You don't like ice cream?

5. Are you hungry? Do you want some bread and cheese?

B. DISCUSS Work with a partner. Take turns asking and answering the questions. Ask follow-up questions if needed. Focus on using the correct intonation.

1. What are your favorite foods?

2. What are three foods you would never try?

3. Who usually cooks at your house?

iQ PRACTICE Go online for more practice with common intonation patterns. *Practice > Unit 5 > Activity 13*

SPEAKING SKILL Expressing interest during a conversation

Expressing interest during a conversation shows the speaker you are paying attention. There are several ways to express interest in the speaker's ideas. In addition to leaning forward and making eye contact, you can use special words and phrases to show you are interested.

> **Encouraging words:** Yeah. / Wow! / Mm-hmm. / Cool!
>
> **Comments:** How interesting! / That's amazing!
>
> **Emphasis questions:** Really?
>
> **Repeating words:** Speaker: I went to Paris. You: Oh, Paris!

It is not necessary to wait until the speaker has finished talking to use these words and phrases. You can use them throughout the conversation, whenever the speaker completes a thought.

 A. APPLY Listen to the conversation between two students who are eating lunch. Fill in the blanks with the words and phrases in the box. Then practice the conversation with a partner.

every day	really	wow
mm-hmm	that's interesting	yeah

Faisal: Hey, Marc. Is this seat free? Do you mind if I sit here?

Marc: Not at all. How are you doing?

Faisal: I'm absolutely starving!

Marc: _____? Why?
    1

Faisal: I went to the gym this morning before school, and by 11:00, my stomach was growling in class.

Marc: _____ , that had to be embarrassing.

2

Faisal: Definitely. So, what did you get for lunch?

Marc: Well, they're serving French onion soup today, so I got some of that. It's not bad, but not like home!

Faisal: _____ ! French food is famous around the world, but I've

3
never had it.

Marc: Well, I am from Provence, in the south of France. People take food very seriously there.

Faisal: _____ .

4

Marc: People buy fresh fruit and vegetables from the market every day.

Faisal: _____ ?

5

Marc: Yeah, and the cheese is amazing! It tastes nothing like what we buy in the grocery stores here.

Faisal: _____ . I feel that way about Saudi Arabian food here, too.

6
It's not quite the same.

B. DISCUSS Work in a group to answer the questions. As you listen, use different ways to express interest and show you are paying attention.

1. What food or drink would you recommend to someone who has a cold? Are there any traditional remedies you use in your family?

2. Which meal is the most important of the day to you? Why?

3. Can you cook? If so, what is a dish that you make particularly well? How do you make it?

iQ PRACTICE Go online for more practice expressing interest during a conversation. *Practice > Unit 5 > Activity 14*

UNIT ASSIGNMENT Take part in a debate

OBJECTIVE ▶

In this assignment, you are going to present your opinions in a debate on food science. As you prepare your opinions, think about the Unit Question, "How has science changed the food we eat?" Use information from Listening 1, Listening 2, and your work in this unit to support your opinions. Refer to the Self-Assessment checklist on page 124.

CONSIDER THE IDEAS

DISCUSS Work in a group. Discuss the photos below. What do you think the advantages and disadvantages of each modification are? Give reasons to support your opinion.

a. Raspberries preserved by radiation, a type of energy that can cause illness in large amounts

b. Raspberries that have not been preserved by radiation

c. A chicken that eats nonchemically treated food

d. A chicken that eats food that has been treated with artificial chemicals to make it grow much larger than normal

PREPARE AND SPEAK

A. GATHER IDEAS Think about the opinions you shared in the Consider the Ideas activity. Which ideas did you find most convincing? Make a short list of the three most convincing opinions on this issue.

B. ORGANIZE IDEAS Create a chart with two columns. Put your list of reasons from Activity A in the first column. In the second column, give details and examples to support each reason.

C. SPEAK Work with a partner who has different opinions on this issue. Take turns presenting your opinions and the reasons that support them. Show interest in your partner's opinions and ask questions to get more information. Refer to the Self-Assessment checklist below before you begin.

iQ PRACTICE Go online for your alternate Unit Assignment.
Practice > Unit 5 > Activity 15

CHECK AND REFLECT

A. CHECK Think about the Unit Assignment as you complete the Self-Assessment checklist.

SELF-ASSESSMENT	Yes	No
I was able to speak easily about the topic.	☐	☐
My partner, group, and class understood me.	☐	☐
I used comparative forms of adjectives and adverbs.	☐	☐
I used vocabulary from the unit.	☐	☐
I expressed interest during the conversation.	☐	☐
I used common intonation patterns correctly.	☐	☐
I evaluated information.	☐	☐

B. REFLECT Discuss these questions with a partner or group.

1. What is something new you learned in this unit?

2. Look back at the Unit Question—How has science changed the food we eat? Is your answer different now than when you started this unit? If yes, how is it different? Why?

iQ PRACTICE Go to the online discussion board to discuss the questions.
Practice > Unit 5 > Activity 16

TRACK YOUR SUCCESS

iQ PRACTICE Go online to check the words and phrases you have learned in this unit. *Practice > Unit 5 > Activity 17*

Check (✓) the skills and strategies you learned. If you need more work on a skill, refer to the page(s) in parentheses.

NOTE-TAKING	☐ I can edit my notes after a lecture. (p. 104)
LISTENING	☐ I can understand bias in a presentation. (p. 109)
CRITICAL THINKING	☐ I can evaluate information for bias. (p. 115)
VOCABULARY	☐ I can recognize and use prefixes and suffixes. (pp. 116)
GRAMMAR	☐ I can use comparative forms of adjectives and adverbs. (p. 118)
PRONUNCIATION	☐ I can use common intonation patterns. (p. 120)
SPEAKING	☐ I can express interest during a conversation. (p. 121)
OBJECTIVE ▶	☐ I can gather information and ideas to participate in a debate on food science.

Education

NOTE-TAKING	comparing and contrasting multiple topics
LISTENING	listening for contrasting ideas
CRITICAL THINKING	ranking options
VOCABULARY	using the dictionary: formal and informal words
GRAMMAR	simple, compound, and complex sentences
PRONUNCIATION	highlighted words
SPEAKING	changing the topic

Is one road to success better than another?

A. Discuss these questions with your classmates.

1. What does being successful mean to you?

2. In your life, have you taken a traditional path or a nontraditional path to reach your educational and career goals? What are the advantages and disadvantages of each path?

3. Look at the photo. What are the people doing? How is teamwork a part of success?

B. Listen to *The Q Classroom* online. Then answer these questions.

1. Marcus thinks that different experiences give workers different perspectives. What is an example of this kind of nontraditional path to success?

2. Felix lists many steps on a traditional road to success: studying hard, getting a degree, getting work experience, getting an entry-level job, and working your way up. Which do you think is the most important step? Why?

iQ PRACTICE   Go to the online discussion board to discuss the Unit Question with your classmates. *Practice > Unit 6 > Activity 1*

UNIT OBJECTIVE

Listen to two conversations, watch a video, and listen to a lecture and gather information and ideas to have a discussion and make a group decision.

When you hear information about related topics, it can be helpful to build a chart so you can easily compare and contrast the main ideas about each topic. Label the columns of your chart with the topics, and label the rows with the examples. Then write notes about each topic in the appropriate box. This is a great way to review and edit your notes after a lecture and to make connections between lectures and readings.

A. CATEGORIZE Listen to the class discussion about nontraditional approaches some businesses have taken to success. Complete the chart.

Company	History	Successes	Problems
Ben and Jerry's	•	•	•
	•	•	•
	•		
	•		
Lululemon	•	•	•
	•		•
	•		
Starbucks	•	•	•
	•		•

B. SYNTHESIZE Use your notes to write a paragraph comparing and contrasting the three companies.

iQ PRACTICE Go online for more practice building a chart to compare and contrast notes on multiple topics. *Practice > Unit 6 > Activity 2*

LISTENING 1 **Failure and Success in Startups**

OBJECTIVE ▶

You are going to listen to a conversation in a business class and then watch a video. As you listen and watch, gather information and ideas about whether one road to success is better than another.

PREVIEW THE LISTENING

A. PREVIEW Before you listen, discuss the questions in a small group.

1. Do you know of anyone who has started their own small business? Were they successful? What kinds of problems have they had?

2. If you tried to start a company and it failed, what would you do? Would you try again? Would you give up? Why?

B. VOCABULARY Read aloud these words from Listening 1. Check (✓) the ones you know. Use a dictionary to define any new or unknown words. Then discuss with a partner how the words will relate to the unit.

burst *(v.)* 🔑	**investor** *(n.)* 🔑	**profit** *(n.)* 🔑
confidence *(n.)* 🔑	**launch** *(v.)* 🔑	**steadily** *(adv.)* 🔑
expand *(v.)* 🔑 OPAL	**massive** *(adj.)* 🔑	**values** *(n.)* 🔑 OPAL
genius *(n.)* 🔑	**pressure** *(n.)* 🔑 OPAL	**vision** *(n.)* 🔑

🔑 Oxford 5000™ words   OPAL Oxford Phrasal Academic Lexicon

iQ PRACTICE Go online to listen and practice your pronunciation.
Practice > Unit 6 > Activity 3

WORK WITH THE LISTENING

iQ RESOURCES Go online to watch the video.
Resources > Video > Unit 6 > Listening 1 Part 2

🔊 **A. LISTEN AND TAKE NOTES** Listen to the conversation. Then watch the video.* Take notes in the chart.

iQ RESOURCES Go online to download extra vocabulary support.
Resources > Extra Vocabulary > Unit 6

Businessperson	History	Problems	Successes
 Scott Nash			
 John Paul DeJoria (right)			
 Michael Acton Smith			

B. RESTATE Work with a partner. Using your notes, take turns telling the story of each businessperson's journey to success.

* Audio version available. *Resources > Audio > Unit 6*

C. DISCUSS Look at your notes. Whose journey to success do you think was the easiest? Whose was the most difficult? Discuss your opinion with a partner. Use your notes to support your opinion.

D. CATEGORIZE Listen and watch again. Read the statements. Write *T* (true) or *F* (false). Then correct each false statement to make it true.

_____ 1. Scott Nash started his business with $700.

_____ 2. Scott Nash delivered food to people from his mother's house.

_____ 3. MOM's Organic Market's profits are around $200,000 every year.

_____ 4. John Paul DeJoria was successful as a door-to-door salesperson from the start.

_____ 5. John Paul DeJoria started a hair products company alone.

_____ 6. John Paul Mitchell Systems sells more than 80 products.

_____ 7. Michael Acton Smith's first business plan was to sell toys, gadgets, and games on the Internet.

_____ 8. Investors in Michael Acton Smith's second business lost £6,000,000.

_____ 9. Michael Acton Smith believes that he would have gotten more money if Moshi Monsters had failed.

_____10. Protecting the environment is important to all three of the businesspeople.

E. INTERPRET Look at the statements. Who might have made them? Write *SN* (Scott Nash), *JPD* (John Paul DeJoria), or *MAS* (Michael Acton Smith).

_____ 1. "Finding investors is an important part of starting a business."

_____ 2. "When you are selling something, you have to be just as excited about the product even after hundreds of doors have closed in your face."

_____ 3. "Meeting the right person early on was essential for my career. I could not have been as good a salesperson without my partner's excellent product."

_____ 4. "Slow growth is strong growth."

_____ 5. "Don't waste a lot of your investors' money on launch events."

_____ 6. "My mother supported me early in my career when I really needed the help."

F. VOCABULARY Here are some words from Listening 1. Complete each sentence with the correct word.

burst *(v.)*	genius *(n.)*	massive *(adj.)*	steadily *(adv.)*
confidence *(n.)*	investor *(n.)*	pressure *(n.)*	values *(n.)*
expand *(v.)*	launch *(v.)*	profit *(n.)*	vision *(n.)*

1. The new car will _____ in July with a big celebration.

2. He is under a lot of _____ at work. I am worried about his health.

3. He is incredibly smart. He might even be a(n) _____.

4. When he was young, he didn't believe in himself, but now he has more

   _____.

5. When people talk about their _____, it's easy to see what is really important to them.

6. When you climb a mountain, you don't want to move too quickly. It's better to go up slowly and _____.

7. That balloon will _____ if you add any more air to it.

8. New companies often put their _____ back into the business so it can continue to grow.

9. I believe the business will _____ into new markets under a new manager.

10. A strong leader needs to have _____ so he or she can see what the future might hold.

11. Her new business needs to look for a(n) _____. They need more money to grow.

12. The government is talking about a _____ increase in spending.

iQ PRACTICE   Go online for more practice with the vocabulary.
Practice > Unit 6 > Activity 4

iQ PRACTICE   Go online for additional listening and comprehension.
Practice > Unit 6 > Activity 5

SAY WHAT YOU THINK

DISCUSS Work in a group to discuss the questions.

1. The businesspeople in the conversation and video understand that failure is a necessary part of success. Why do they believe this is true? Do you agree? Why or why not?

2. Were you surprised by the challenges these people experienced? Explain.

LISTENING SKILL Listening for contrasting ideas

When speakers **contrast** things or ideas, they use special words and phrases to point out different characteristics of the things being discussed.

The simplest way to show a contrast is to use a comparative adjective + *than*.

⌐ He became a **better** salesperson **than** he was before.

Speakers also contrast things and ideas by using words and phrases such as *in contrast to, instead of, however, on the other hand, but, rather than,* and *whereas.*

⌐ **In contrast to** Scott Nash, John Paul DeJoria wasn't a very successful salesperson at the start.

So, sometimes entrepreneurs start small and steadily grow. **But** more often, starting a new business is a journey of mistakes and failures.

 A. APPLY Listen to a discussion about two candidates for a job. Fill in the blanks with the contrasting words and phrases you hear.

TIP FOR SUCCESS

To understand a speaker's meaning, it's important to analyze the words and phrases they use. The way a speaker organizes and presents information is usually an important clue about what the speaker wants you to know.

Mr. Doshi: Bob Quintero and Susan Miyamoto are the final candidates for the marketing position at our company. Bob has a degree from Harvard University in the USA, _____1_____ Susan has a degree from Keio Business School in Japan.

Ms. Stanz: Bob and Susan both have good work experience. Bob has worked for five years at a small marketing company. _____2_____ Susan has worked for eight years at our company.

Mr. Doshi: Susan speaks more languages. Bob speaks Arabic and Spanish. _____3_____, Susan speaks French, Spanish, and Japanese.

Ms. Stanz: Bob has a lot of sales experience. _____4_____, Susan has a lot of experience at our company.

Mr Doshi: Hmmm. This is going to be a tough decision!

B. CATEGORIZE Listen to the conversation and watch the video from Listening 1 again. As you listen and watch, check (✓) the person or people each statement describes.

	Scott Nash	John Paul DeJoria	Michael Acton Smith
Started a business with a little money			
Started a business with a lot of money from investors			
Expanded his company slowly			
Learned from his early failures			
Failed because he spent too much money			
Focused on his values			
Failed two times before he succeeded			

C. COMPOSE Work with a partner. Take turns making sentences that compare Scott Nash, John Paul DeJoria, and Michael Acton Smith using words and phrases to show contrast.

in contrast to	instead of	however	on the other hand
but	rather than	whereas	

iQ PRACTICE Go online for more practice listening for contrasting ideas.
Practice > Unit 6 > Activity 6

LISTENING 2 Interns in New York

OBJECTIVE ▶

You are going to listen to a lecture and then listen to a conversation between two friends about the advantages and disadvantages of doing an internship. As you listen, gather information and ideas about whether one road to success is better than another.

PREVIEW THE LISTENING

A. PREVIEW An internship is work experience available to students and new graduates for a short period of time. The interns are sometimes not paid or paid very little. Discuss the questions in a small group.

1. Would you consider working for free in order to learn more about a job you might want to do in the future? If yes, what job would you like to try?

2. Do you know of anyone who has done an internship? What was his or her experience like?

B. VOCABULARY Read aloud these words from Listening 2. Check (✓) the ones you know. Use a dictionary to define any new or unknown words. Then discuss with a partner how the words will relate to the unit.

altogether *(adv.)* 🔑	in particular *(idm)* 🔑 OPAL
basically *(adv.)* 🔑 OPAL	meaningful *(adj.)* 🔑 OPAL
decent *(adj.)* 🔑	miserable *(adj.)* 🔑
disposable *(adj.)*	predecessor *(n.)* 🔑
fairness *(n.)* 🔑	rate *(n.)* 🔑 OPAL
fierce *(adj.)* 🔑	workforce *(n.)* 🔑

🔑 Oxford 5000™ words   OPAL Oxford Phrasal Academic Lexicon

iQ PRACTICE Go online to listen and practice your pronunciation.
Practice › Unit 6 › Activity 7

WORK WITH THE LISTENING

 A. LISTEN AND TAKE NOTES Listen to the lecture and the conversation. In the chart, list advantages and disadvantages of doing an internship.

iQ RESOURCES Go online to download extra vocabulary support.
Resources > Extra Vocabulary > Unit 6

Advantages of an internship	Disadvantages of an internship

B. EVALUATE In the Listening, HyoJin is talking with a friend, Nicholas. Do you think HyoJin's summer plans sound better than Nicholas's? Use your notes to explain your choice to a partner.

C. IDENTIFY Check (✓) the solutions to the problem of unpaid internships that are mentioned in Listening 2.

_____ 1. sue the employer

_____ 2. create a union to reject unpaid internships

_____ 3. reduce the unemployment rate

_____ 4. complain to the government

_____ 5. write a letter to the management

D. IDENTIFY Read the questions. Then listen again. Circle the correct answers.

1. Why did Lucy Bickerton sue the company where she did her internship?

   a. Because she had to work too many hours every day

   b. Because she wasn't paid, even though she was doing a real job

   c. Because the company didn't hire her after she did the internship

2. What do the groups Intern Aware and the Global Intern Coalition do?

   a. Help match interns and companies

   b. Sue companies so they pay the interns

   c. Work to improve conditions for interns

3. According to the lecture, what was the unemployment rate for young people last year?

    a. 12.5%

    b. 20%

    c. 24%

4. How did HyoJin's brother benefit from his internship?

    a. He learned how to work at a big company.

    b. He was more competitive when he applied at other tech companies.

    c. He met people in the tech industry who helped him start his own company.

5. Why might HyoJin choose to take the unpaid internship?

    a. It would not be hot, dirty, or hard work.

    b. The projects will be interesting and meaningful.

    c. It will make her more competitive for other jobs.

E. **RESTATE** HyoJin's brother and sister had very different internship experiences. Work with a partner. Imagine and discuss what advice they might give HyoJin.

HyoJin's brother: "_____"

HyoJin's sister: "_____"

F. **DISCUSS** Work in a small group to discuss the questions.

1. Would internships work better in some industries than in others? What are some workplaces that would be more accommodating to interns? What are some that would not be? Why?

2. Interns are typically younger people in their early 20s. However, older workers who are changing their careers might also be interns. Are there any advantages or disadvantages to hiring an older intern? If you were a manager of a company, would you prefer to hire an older or a younger intern? Why?

3. Think of a company you might like to work at in the future. What would you be able to learn as an intern? What kinds of tasks would you do?

VOCABULARY SKILL REVIEW

In Unit 5, you learned to use prefixes and suffixes to help determine the meaning of new vocabulary words. Identify two words containing a suffix used for adverbs in Activity G.

G. VOCABULARY Here are some words from Listening 2. Read the sentences. Then write each bold word next to the correct definition.

1. When I started my new job, I changed many of the policies of my **predecessor**.

2. It is completely wrong for corporations to view workers as **disposable.**

3. I want a job that I like, but it's also important to make a **decent** salary. I need to pay rent and buy food.

4. The new leader wanted to make **meaningful** changes that would make life better for her country.

5. The pay **rate** for new employees is usually not very good.

6. He wanted to quit smoking **altogether**.

7. She has strong ideas about justice and **fairness**. She should be a judge.

8. There are more men in the **workforce** than women right now.

9. I hated my job and my boss was angry all the time. Going to work every day was a **miserable** experience.

10. The competition between the two athletes was **fierce**, and the results were very close.

11. She had some problems at her new school, but **basically,** she likes it.

12. Do you like any music **in particular**, or do you listen to all music?

a. _____ (adv.) completely

b. _____ (adj.) showing strong feelings or a lot of activity

c. _____ (adj.) of a good enough standard or quality

d. _____ (adj.) unpleasant

e. _____ (idm.) special, specific

f. _____ (n.) the people who are available for work

g. _____ (adj.) serious or important

h. _____ (adv.) in the most important ways; essentially

i. _____ (n.) a person who did a job before someone else

j. _____ (n.) treating people equally

k. _____ (adj.) that you can easily stop employing or thinking about

l. _____ (n.) an amount of money that is charged or paid for something

iQ PRACTICE Go online for more practice with the vocabulary.
Practice > Unit 6 > Activity 8

CRITICAL THINKING STRATEGY

Ranking options

Ranking helps you make decisions when you have to choose between several options. When you rank things in a group, you first need to decide which characteristics are positive and which are negative. Then you make a judgment about each option—whether it has enough advantages and not too many disadvantages. Finally, you compare each option with the other options and you put them in order, usually from what you most prefer to what you least prefer. Make sure you know why you ranked it that way.

iQ PRACTICE Go online to watch the Critical Thinking Video and check your comprehension. *Practice > Unit 6 > Activity 9*

H. EXTEND Consider the following work experience opportunities. Which opportunity would you prefer? Rank the options. Think about your choices and try to list a few reasons why you ranked them the way you did.

____ an internship at a large tech company

____ an internship at a museum

____ an internship at a small, grassroots nonprofit organization

____ an internship with a large, well-known nonprofit organization

____ working for pay in a family business

I. DISCUSS Share your list with a partner. Explain the reasons for your rankings.

SAY WHAT YOU THINK

SYNTHESIZE Think about Listening 1 and Listening 2 as you discuss the questions.

1. Would you prefer to start your own business, like the businesspeople in Listening 1, or work for an established company, like the interns in Listening 2? Why?

2. In Listening 1, the businesspeople learned from mistakes they made. In Listening 2, the interns learned from working with people who were more experienced than they were. In your opinion, which way is better? How would you prefer to learn?

VOCABULARY SKILL Using the dictionary: formal and informal words

English does not have strong rules of formality like some languages do. However, in some situations, it may be more appropriate to use certain words than others. In other more casual situations, it may be more appropriate to use less formal vocabulary, such as *phrasal verbs* and *idioms*. It is helpful to know when to use certain words and phrases.

A dictionary can guide you on which word to use. It will tell you if a word is informal or slang. If a definition doesn't say this, you can usually assume it is more formal or neutral.

Here are some examples.

> **PHR V** ˌhang aˈround (…) (*informal*) to wait or stay near a place, not doing very much: *You hang around here in case he comes, and I'll go on ahead.* ˌhang aˈround with sb (*informal*) to spend a lot of time with someone ˌhang ˈback to remain

> those old photos—they may be valuable. ˌhang ˈout (*informal*) to spend a lot of time in a place: *The local kids hang out at the mall.* ➲ related noun HANGOUT ˌhang ˈout with sb (*informal*)

> so·cial·ize /ˈsoʊʃəˌlaɪz/ *verb* **1** [I] ~ (**with sb**) to meet and spend time with people in a friendly way, in order to enjoy yourself **SYN** MIX: *I enjoy socializing with the other students.*
> ◆ *Maybe you should socialize more.* **2** [T, often passive] ~ **sb**

The dictionary categorizes *hang around* and *hang out* as informal, but *socialize* has no description like this.

Here are some examples of appropriate use.

> **To your friends:** I'll be <u>hanging around</u> all day.
> **To your family:** I'm going to <u>hang out</u> with my friends today.
> **In a presentation:** Most teenagers enjoy <u>socializing</u> with friends.

All dictionary entries adapted from the *Oxford Advanced American Dictionary for learners of English* © Oxford University Press 2011.

A. IDENTIFY Read the pairs of sentences. Check (✓) the sentence that sounds more formal.

1. ☐ a. I can always **count on** you to help me out.
   ✓ b. I always **trust** that you'll assist me.

2. ☐ a. My brother must **select** a new suit for his interview.
   ☐ b. My brother has to **pick out** a new suit for his interview.

3. ☐ a. Lately I've been **enthusiastic about** volunteering.
   ☐ b. These days I'm really **into** the idea of volunteering.

4. ☐ a. I have to **cut back** on my work hours this semester.
   ☐ b. I have to **reduce** the number of hours I work this semester.

B. IDENTIFY Read the sentences. Circle the answer that means almost the same as the bold word in each sentence.

1. I don't think we need to **hang around** here until he returns.

    a. wait   b. climb   c. joke

2. He was hoping to **get** a promotion at work.

    a. find   b. receive   c. give

3. You don't need to **put up with** a job that is so boring! Get a new one.

    a. tolerate   b. look for   c. create

4. Have you **looked into** other companies to work for? There must be many others like that one.

    a. answered   b. counted   c. researched

5. **Jumping up** a few steps at a time is almost impossible in a traditional career path.

    a. bouncing   b. advancing   c. returning

6. I've been working so hard at school. I'm **worn out**. I need to rest!

    a. prepared   b. tired   c. worried

C. APPLY Circle the appropriate synonym to complete each sentence. Then work with a partner to read the conversations.

Interviewee: Good morning. I'm here to (have a word / speak) with Ms. Lee.
                                                                    1

Receptionist: Please (wait / hang around) here. I'll tell Ms. Lee you're here.
                                   2

Ms. Lee: Good morning. So let's (get going / begin). Can you tell me why you'd
                                              3
like to work for this company?

Interviewee: Well, I'm really (interested in / into) your products.
                                           4

iQ PRACTICE Go online for more practice using the dictionary to identify formal and informal words. *Practice > Unit 6 > Activity 10*

SPEAKING

OBJECTIVE ▶ At the end of this unit, you are going to participate in a group discussion about the qualifications of job applicants and make a hiring decision. Throughout the discussion, you will need to be able to change the topic.

GRAMMAR Simple, compound, and complex sentences

Using a variety of sentence types will allow you to express a range of ideas in your speeches and presentations.

There are three basic kinds of sentences: **simple**, **compound**, and **complex**.

A **simple sentence** is one independent clause (one subject + verb combination) that makes sense by itself.

I want to do research.
subject verb

A **compound sentence** is made of at least two independent clauses joined together with a conjunction, such as *and, but, or, yet*, and *so*.

independent clause   independent clause
Paul had quality hair products to sell, **and** John Paul was a good salesman.
conjunction

A **complex sentence** is made of at least one independent clause and one dependent clause. A dependent clause is not a complete idea by itself. The dependent clause begins with a subordinating conjunction, such as *because*, *before*, *since*, *after*, *although*, *if*, or *when*.

independent clause   dependent clause
I might learn a lot **if** I'm lucky and get hired by a good company.
subordinating conjunction

If the dependent clause comes before the independent clause, then a comma separates the two clauses.

Although she was an unpaid intern, she was doing the work of a full-time production assistant.

iQ RESOURCES Go online to watch the Grammar Skill Video.
Resources ⟩ Video ⟩ Unit 6 ⟩ Grammar Skill Video

A. IDENTIFY Read each sentence. Is the sentence simple, compound, or complex? Circle the correct answer. Then compare answers with a partner.

1. This model is similar to the business cultures in other countries.

   (simple / compound / complex)

2. The right training is important, but what other steps do you need to take to reach your career goal?

(simple / compound / complex)

3. Because he moved in and out of companies as positions opened, he could advance faster toward his career goal.

(simple / compound / complex)

4. Many countries in Asia follow this business model.

(simple / compound / complex)

5. After she worked for a year, she was ready to return to school.

(simple / compound / complex)

B. RESTATE Rewrite the conversation below. Combine the simple sentences using the words in parentheses. Then practice the conversation.

Sam was walking down the street. He saw his friend Inez. (when)

Sam was walking down the street when he saw his friend Inez.

Inez: Hey, Sam! How did your job interview go?

Sam: Hi! It went really well. I might get the job! (and)

Inez: That's great! When will you know for sure?

Sam: They'll make the decision this afternoon. They'll call me. (after)

Inez: Good luck! By the way, did you hear about Adam?

Sam: No. I sent him an email last week. He hasn't answered it. (but)

Inez: Well, he's taking a year off. He's going to Antarctica to study penguins. (because)

Sam: Wow! That sounds amazing.

Inez: Yeah. It seems like an incredible opportunity. I can't imagine living in Antarctica. (although)

Sam: What about you? How are you going to spend the summer?

Inez: I applied to two programs. I might volunteer for a group that builds houses for people. I might work in a program for street kids. (or)

Sam: Those both sound like important projects! They'll look good on your college application. (and)

Inez: Yeah. I need to do something significant. I want to get into a good school! (if)

Sam: Well, I should get home. I can wait for the call about the job. (so)

Inez: See you later!

iQ PRACTICE Go online for more practice with simple, compound, and complex sentences. *Practice > Unit 6 > Activities 11–12*

PRONUNCIATION Highlighted words

Speakers typically use a higher pitch and longer vowel sounds to emphasize or highlight content words.

For example, a speaker might stress the words in the following sentence normally.

   ⌐ He <u>started</u> his <u>business</u> with <u>only one hundred dollars</u>.

Sometimes a speaker will shift the stress from this regular stress pattern to emphasize an idea. **Highlighted words** often present a contrast or a correction.

A speaker who wants to emphasize the amount of money the business started with might place a heavier stress on *one hundred*.

⌐ He <u>started</u> his <u>business</u> with <u>only</u> **one hundred** <u>dollars</u>.
∟ (meaning = not two hundred dollars)

Or, if the speaker wants to correct the idea that someone else started the business, he or she might stress *he*.

⌐ **He** <u>started</u> his <u>business</u> with <u>only one hundred dollars</u>.
∟ (meaning = not someone else)

Any word can be highlighted. It's important to listen for and use highlighted words carefully because they change the meaning of the sentence.

A. IDENTIFY Listen to each sentence. Underline the highlighted words you hear. Then practice saying the sentences with a partner.

1. I would love to do an internship at a major tech company.

2. If I had to pick just one place to work, it would be New York City.

3. When Carlos was there, they didn't have the internship program.

4. She's working at a new engineering company.

5. You'll learn a lot while you're there, and you'll have so much fun!

B. INTERPRET Listen to each sentence. What is the speaker's meaning? Circle the correct answers.

1. I would like to get a job in Zambia working with wild animals.

    a. I am interested in Zambia.

    b. I hope I have a good chance at getting the job.

    c. I'm more interested in wild animals than domestic animals.

2. I change jobs often. My father's career path was more traditional.

    a. My career path is different from my father's career path.

    b. I like to change jobs to help my career.

    c. I prefer traditional career paths.

3. I think I can build skills for this career if I take a year off to study.

    a. I'm not sure I can build my skills.

    b. I can only build skills by taking time off.

    c. If I take a year off, I have to study the whole time.

4. The best reason to do an internship is the chance to learn about yourself.

    a. This reason is very important.

    b. Learning is very important.

    c. You are very important.

5. No one ever told me that the group would leave before school is over.

    a. I expected the group to stay at the school.

    b. I thought the group would leave after school is over.

    c. They told other people, but they forgot to tell me.

C. APPLY Work with a partner. Practice the conversation. Stress the bold words.

A: Have you heard about Lee's **latest** plan?

B: No. What does he want to do **now**?

A: He says he **finally** decided to do an internship in a government office.

B: He wants to **do an internship**? I thought he wanted a paying job.

A: Well, it seems he changed his mind **again**.

B: Hmm. He **would** be good at it. He's a natural leader.

A: He's good at **lots** of things, so I'm sure he'll think of more ideas.

B: Yeah. He probably won't figure out where to work until **right** before he leaves!

iQ PRACTICE Go online for more practice with highlighted words.
Practice > Unit 6 > Activity 13

In the middle of a conversation you may want to **change the topic** a little. However, you don't want to sound like you are uninterested in what someone else is saying. To let someone know you want to add something related to the topic, you can use *transition phrases*. Here are some examples:

> By the way . . .
>
> Speaking of (previous topic) . . .
>
> That reminds me . . .

For example, if your friend is talking about a book he finished reading yesterday, you can say, "Oh, speaking of books, did you hear about that new adventure novel?"

Sometimes you remember something in the middle of a conversation that is not at all related to the current topic. It is important to let others know you are about to switch to an unrelated topic. Here are some expressions you can use:

> Hold that thought.
>
> Oh, before I forget . . .
>
> Oh, I wanted to tell / ask you . . .

For example, you and two friends are talking about an exhibition. You suddenly remember you wanted to ask them about an important class project. You wait for a short pause in the conversation and then say, "Oh, before I forget, I wanted to ask you if you want to go over the project notes today."

To return to the previous topic, you can then use phrases like these:

> But you were saying . . .
>
> Back to (the topic) . . .
>
> Anyway . . .

A. APPLY Complete the conversation with the words you hear. Then practice the conversation with a partner.

A: I've had a very long day. I just came from my job.

B: _____, I need to get your résumé. My company is
   hiring, and you would be perfect for the position.

A: Really? That's great! You make your job sound fun.

B: It is, most of the time. We all get along well at work.

A: Oh, _____ if you have time to help me with
   my homework.

B: Sure I can. We'll do it after class.

A: _____, I'd love to give you my résumé. I've been
     looking for a new job.
                        3

B: I know. _____, my boss says she's interviewing
                                          4
     people next week. Are you free in the morning?

A: I'll make sure I'm available if she calls me.

B: _____. I have to get to my next class. We'll talk
     about this later.
                  5

A: See you.

B. EXTEND Work in a group. Discuss the questions. Practice changing and
returning to topics.

1. What does it mean to be successful? How do you define it for yourself?

2. What are the characteristics of a dream job? What steps should someone
    take—traditional and nontraditional—to get their dream job?

3. What type of person is most likely to achieve his or her dream job?

iQ PRACTICE Go online for more practice changing the topic.
Practice > Unit 6 > Activity 14

UNIT ASSIGNMENT
OBJECTIVE ▶

Reach a group decision

In this assignment, you are going to have a discussion in order to reach a group
decision. As you prepare for your discussion, think about the Unit Question, "Is one
road to success better than another?" Use information from Listening 1, Listening 2,
and your work in this unit to support your discussion. Refer to the Self-Assessment
checklist on page 150.

CONSIDER THE IDEAS

Complete the activities.

1. Read the following advertisement for a job opening.

GapStaff is looking for a consultant to join our exciting and energetic team. Consultants are responsible for working with clients to organize their gap year opportunities. Candidates for the job should be well organized, interesting in working with students, and passionate about traveling, learning, and volunteering.

The minimum requirements for the position are an undergraduate degree and five years of related work experience.
Travel experience and the ability to speak another language are a plus.

2. Read the information about four people who applied for the GapStaff consultant job. Then listen to their personal statements. Take notes in the chart.

Personal information	Notes
Susan Jones (age 59) **Education:** A.A. in Journalism from Central Texas College B.A. in English from the University of Chicago **Work Experience:** English teacher in Poland (3 years) English teacher in Morocco (2 years) English teacher in Peru (6 years)	
Doug Orman (age 43) **Education:** B.A. in History from the University of Maryland M.A. in History from the University of Maryland **Work Experience:** Teaching Assistant at the University of Maryland (3 years) Lecturer at the University of Maryland (16 years)	

Personal information	Notes

Narayan Tej (age 24)
Education:
  B.A. in Tourism from Columbia Southern University
Work Experience:
  Part-time work at the tourism desk of the Hilton Hotel	

Teresa Lopez (age 35)
Education:
  B.S. in Business Administration from National
  American University
Work Experience:
  Guide at local museum (3 years)
  Receptionist for travel agent (2 years)
  Receptionist for gym (5 years)
  Salesperson at clothing store (2 years)	

PREPARE AND SPEAK

A. GATHER IDEAS Imagine you are part of a GapStaff group choosing the best candidate for the position. Consider the four job applicants. Who do you think is most qualified? Who is least qualified? Rank the applicants from 1 (your first choice) to 4 (your last choice), based on your notes in the chart above.

____ Susan Jones   ____ Narayan Tej

____ Doug Orman   ____ Teresa Lopez

B. ORGANIZE IDEAS Why did you rank the candidates in this order? Complete the chart with brief notes.

Candidate name	Reasons for ranking
1.	
2.	
3.	
4.	

C. SPEAK Work in a group. Discuss who should be hired for the position. Share your reasons with the group. Work to reach a group decision on the best person to hire. Refer to the Self-Assessment checklist below before you begin.

iQ PRACTICE Go online for your alternate Unit Assignment.
Practice > Unit 6 > Activity 15

CHECK AND REFLECT

A. CHECK Think about the Unit Assignment as you complete the Self-Assessment checklist.

SELF-ASSESSMENT	Yes	No
I was able to speak easily about the topic.	☐	☐
My partner, group, and class understood me.	☐	☐
I listened for contrasting ideas.	☐	☐
I used vocabulary from the unit.	☐	☐
I changed the topic in the discussion.	☐	☐
I highlighted words to emphasize ideas as I spoke.	☐	☐
I ranked options.	☐	☐

B. REFLECT Discuss these questions with a partner or group.

1. What is something new you learned in this unit?

2. Look back at the Unit Question—Is one road to success better than another? Is your answer different now than when you started this unit? If yes, how is it different? Why?

iQ PRACTICE Go to the online discussion board to discuss the questions.
Practice > Unit 6 > Activity 16

TRACK YOUR SUCCESS

iQ PRACTICE Go online to check the words and phrases you have learned in this unit. *Practice > Unit 6 > Activity 17*

Check (✓) the skills and strategies you learned. If you need more work on a skill, refer to the page(s) in parentheses.

NOTE-TAKING	☐ I can compare and contrast multiple topics. (p. 128)
LISTENING	☐ I can listen for contrasting ideas. (p. 133)
CRITICAL THINKING	☐ I can rank options based on advantages and disadvantages. (p. 139)
VOCABULARY	☐ I can use the dictionary to find formal or informal words. (p. 140)
GRAMMAR	☐ I can use simple, compound, and complex sentences. (p. 142)
PRONUNCIATION	☐ I can highlight words to emphasize ideas. (p. 144)
SPEAKING	☐ I can change the topic. (p. 146)

OBJECTIVE ▶ ☐ I can gather information and ideas to have a discussion in order to reach a group decision.

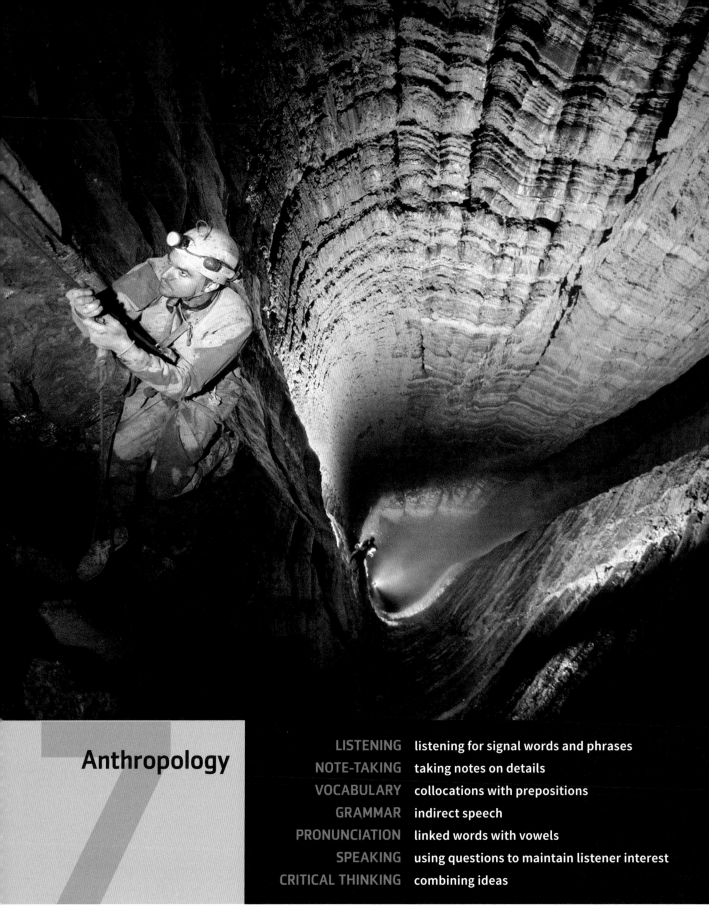

Anthropology

How can accidental discoveries affect our lives?

A. Discuss these questions with your classmates.

1. The journalist Franklin Adams once wrote, "I find that a great part of the information I have was acquired by looking up something and finding something else on the way." What do you think he meant?

2. Have you ever discovered something important by accident? If so, what was it? How did the discovery affect you?

3. Look at the photo. Why might this place be a good space for an accidental discovery? What might you discover in a place like this?

B. Listen to *The Q Classroom* online. Then answer these questions.

1. Marcus says that it is important to keep learning and having new experiences. Do you agree with him? What does his advice have to do with making accidental discoveries?

2. Each student talks about accidental discoveries in a very positive way. Do you think there are some situations where accidental discoveries aren't so positive? If so, in what situations?

iQ PRACTICE Go to the online discussion board to discuss the Unit Question with your classmates. *Practice > Unit 7 > Activity 1*

UNIT OBJECTIVE

Listen to two reports and gather information and ideas to tell a personal story about an accidental discovery you made and how it affected you.

LISTENING 1

OBJECTIVE ▶

The Power of Serendipity

You are going to listen to a news report about how accidental discoveries have led to some important scientific developments. As you listen to the report, gather information and ideas about how accidental discoveries can affect our lives.

PREVIEW THE LISTENING

A. PREVIEW Scientists work hard to keep control of their work and make sure mistakes do not happen. How often do you think accidents play a role in scientific discoveries? Discuss with a partner.

B. VOCABULARY Read aloud these words from Listening 1. Check (✓) the ones you know. Use a dictionary to define any new or unknown words. Then discuss with a partner how the words will relate to the unit.

adhesive *(n.)*	inconceivable *(adj.)*	synthetic *(adj.)*
exploit *(v.)* 🔑 OPAL	interact *(v.)* 🔑 OPAL	unreliable *(adj.)*
flammable *(adj.)*	mandatory *(adj.)* 🔑	vastly *(adv.)*
inadvertent *(adj.)*	obvious *(adj.)* 🔑 OPAL	

🔑 Oxford 5000™ words   OPAL Oxford Phrasal Academic Lexicon

iQ PRACTICE Go online to listen and practice your pronunciation.
Practice > Unit 7 > Activity 2

WORK WITH THE LISTENING

🔊 **A. LISTEN AND TAKE NOTES** Take notes about the main ideas and important details you hear.

Main ideas	Important details

B. CREATE Review your notes from Activity A and write questions in the section on the left. These can be questions your teacher might ask, questions answered in the listening, or other questions you would like to find answers to. Then compare your notes and questions with a partner.

🔊 **C. IDENTIFY** Use your notes to match each scientific breakthrough with the accident or event that led to it. Then listen again to check your answers.

Accident or Event

____ 1. Alfred Nobel worked with a flammable medicine.

____ 2. A sticky substance was mixed with sulfur and dropped on a hot stove.

____ 3. An Ethiopian goat herder watched his goats eating.

____ 4. Nomads traveled on camels carrying milk in stomach bags.

____ 5. A scientist tried to invent a new form of adhesive, but it was very weak.

____ 6. Scientists tried to create synthetic rubber but failed.

Scientific Breakthrough

a. The effects of coffee beans were discovered.

b. Rubber became a useful product.

c. Cheese was made for the first time.

d. Dynamite was discovered.

e. Silly Putty® was invented.

f. Post-it Notes® were invented.

D. CATEGORIZE Read the statements. Write *T* (true) or *F* (false). Then correct each false statement to make it true.

___ 1. Serendipity is looking for one thing and finding something more valuable by accident.

___ 2. Food serendipity has little to do with animals.

___ 3. Serendipity rarely plays a role in products we purchase today.

___ 4. Serendipity is a source of innovation.

___ 5. According to one of the speakers, serendipity is a luxury that is nice but not necessary.

E. EXTEND Which items do you think were discovered or invented by accident? Compare your choices with a partner. Then conduct some research to find out if your choices are correct.

chocolate chip cookies

rechargeable batteries

tea

the pacemaker

Velcro®

Global Positioning System (GPS)

F. VOCABULARY Here are some words from Listening 1. Read the sentences. Circle the answer that best matches the meaning of each bold word.

1. Please keep **flammable** objects away from the stove. It isn't safe while we're cooking.

    a. easily breaks   b. easily burns

2. My car is **unreliable**. I often take the bus to work because my car won't start.

    a. cannot be depended on   b. cannot be understood

3. Miteb made an **inadvertent** discovery as he drove to the airport. He took the wrong exit, turned left, and was at the airport. Now he knows a faster route!

    a. not done on purpose   b. not important to remember

4. Solar energy is a great source of power but not enough people use it. We must learn to **exploit** it more fully.

    a. to use something for benefit   b. to save something

5. There is an **obvious** connection between getting overtired and getting sick.

    a. hard to understand   b. easy to see

6. We need a strong **adhesive** to hang the poster on the wall. Otherwise, the poster will just fall off.

    a. glue   b. surface

7. Not long ago, there was no wireless communication. But now, living without it is **inconceivable** for many people.

    a. hard to find   b. hard to imagine

8. Nawaf and I have **vastly** different taste in clothes.

    a. hardly   b. very greatly

9. Many people like to use websites to **interact** with people that have similar interests.

    a. get contact information   b. communicate

10. Attendance at our monthly meetings is **mandatory**. Everyone must attend.

    a. exciting   b. required

11. According to my auto mechanic, **synthetic** oil is better for my car than regular oil. He says man-made oil lasts longer.

    a. not natural   b. not expensive

iQ PRACTICE Go online for more practice with the vocabulary.
Practice > Unit 7 > Activity 3

iQ PRACTICE Go online for additional listening and comprehension.
Practice > Unit 7 > Activity 4

? SAY WHAT YOU THINK

DISCUSS Work in a group to discuss the questions.

1. Several of the products mentioned in the report were invented by scientists who were working hard to invent something else. What do you think this tells us about serendipity?

2. Some of the research and experiments mentioned in the report are paid for by businesses. Do you think this is a wise investment for the businesses? Why or why not?

3. One speaker in the report says serendipity is mandatory. Do you agree with this? Give reasons to support your answer.

LISTENING SKILL Listening for signal words and phrases

When you are listening to a speaker and hear a word you don't recognize, continue listening for a definition. Sometimes, speakers will give the meaning of a word they just used. Good speakers use **signal words and phrases** to clarify what they mean. Here are some examples.

This refers to . . .	What I mean by ____ is . . .
This means . . .	What is ____? It's . . .
A(n) ____ is . . .	____, or ____, . . .

Sometimes speakers say the same idea in a different way to make the meaning clear. Here are some ways that speakers signal they are about to provide an explanation.

| What I mean is . . . | Here's what this means . . . |
| In other words . . . | In simpler terms, this means . . . |

Listening for signals like these will help you to understand important words and concepts that speakers introduce.

 A. APPLY Read and listen to the lecture. Fill in the blanks with the signal words and phrases you hear.

Professor: Many people use a microwave oven every day. How many of you know that the microwave oven was the result of an accident?

During World War II, scientists invented the magnetron, _____ a kind of
₁
electronic tube that produces microwaves. We're all familiar with microwave ovens,

but _____ a microwave? Well, it's a very short electromagnetic wave.
₂

a magnetron

Anyway, in 1946, an engineer named Dr. Percy Spencer was standing close to a magnetron he was testing. He suddenly noticed something unusual. He felt something warm in his shirt pocket. He reached in and discovered that the candy bar in his pocket was a hot, chocolaty mess. _____,
the candy bar had melted. Dr. Spencer was so excited because he realized that microwaves could raise the internal temperature of food.

_____, microwaves were able to cook food from the inside out! And do it very quickly.

Dr. Spencer saw the possibilities here. His next step was to build a metal box into which he fed microwave power that couldn't escape. He put various foods inside the metal box and tested cooking them. In time, he invented something that would revolutionize cooking—the ubiquitous microwave oven. By that _____ that we see microwave ovens just about everywhere.

B. IDENTIFY Read the sentences. Complete each sentence with a signal word or phrase from the Listening Skill box. Then practice reading the sentences with a partner.

1. It was all by accident. _____
   the invention was the result of serendipity.

2. There were endless possibilities. _____
   _____ the new discovery could be used for many different things.

3. Then a light bulb went off. _____
   I realized what I had to do to make it work correctly.

4. It was a stupendous success. _____
   _____ it worked better than anyone had hoped.

5. Soon it will be commonplace. _____
   _____ everyone will own one and love it!

"A light bulb went off."

iQ PRACTICE Go online for more practice listening for signal words and phrases. *Practice > Unit 7 > Activity 5*

When you take notes on a report or a story, write down details that are important to the account. Try to list specific names and dates, along with major events and their effects. Do not try to write complete sentences. Instead, just write down key words and phrases to help you remember the details. When you review your notes, the list of details will provide you with a kind of timeline and will help you recall the major people, events, and facts.

 A. IDENTIFY Listen and read the account of a major archaeological discovery. Take notes on the important details that make up the story.

A Walk to Remember

The year was 1940, and Marcel Ravidat was a French 18-year-old. One day he did what he often liked to do. He went for a walk in the woods near his home. He was with two friends and his dog, Robot. They had strolled along those same trails many times, but this day would be different. Marcel would stumble upon something amazing.

Actually, you could say that Robot literally stumbled upon it. Some say that as the group was walking through the woods, the little dog ran off. Marcel and his friends ran after it, trying to keep up. When they finally caught up to Robot, they found him digging down into a hole that had been left by a collapsed tree. And for some reason Marcel began to help Robot dig. He didn't realize that he was about to make a huge archaeological discovery.

The hole he was digging turned out to lead to a system of caves. Marcel climbed down into the cave through the widened hole, and there he found a series of prehistoric wall paintings. There were many of them, and they depicted animals—bulls, horses, and deer—in bright colors.

The discovery became a major news event. Researchers were amazed by it, and tourists flocked to the site from around the world. In fact, so many people visited the cave that in 1963 it had to be closed off again to protect the paintings.

Marcel's discovery was as historic as it was unexpected. When he headed out into those familiar woods that morning, he had no idea that he would find a passageway to another time, to another world.

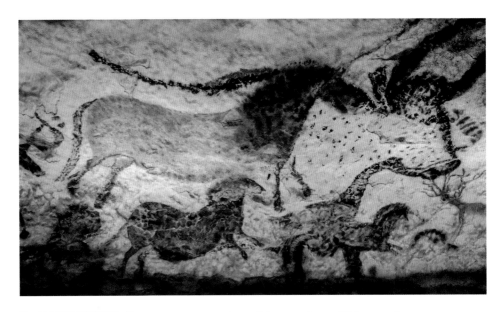

B. **CATEGORIZE** Compare your notes with a partner. Did you miss any important details? Did you list any details that you now think are unnecessary? Use your notes to make a timeline of the main events in the story.

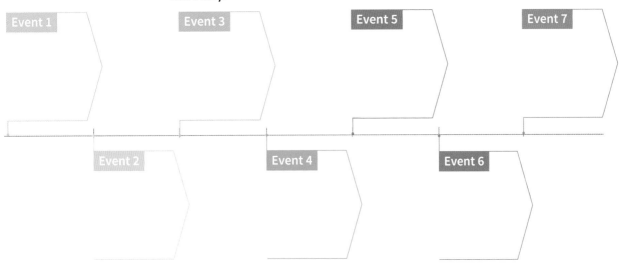

Event 1

Event 2

Event 3

Event 4

Event 5

Event 6

Event 7

iQ PRACTICE Go online for more practice taking notes on details.
Practice > Unit 7 > Activity 6

Against All Odds, Twin Girls Reunited

OBJECTIVE ▶

You are going to listen to a report about how twins were reunited unexpectedly. As you listen to the report, gather information and ideas about how accidental discoveries can affect our lives.

PREVIEW THE LISTENING

A. PREVIEW If two siblings were separated as babies and then met many years later, do you think they would still feel an emotional connection? Check (✓) *yes* or *no*. Discuss your answer with a partner.

☐ yes ☐ no

B. VOCABULARY Read aloud these words from Listening 2. Check (✓) the ones you know. Use a dictionary to define any new or unknown words. Then discuss with a partner how the words will relate to the unit.

ache *(v.)*	biological *(adj.)* 🔑	in all probability *(adv. phr.)*
adopt *(v.)* 🔑 OPAL	deprived *(adj.)*	odds *(n.)* 🔑
alert *(adj.)* 🔑	face to face *(adv. phr.)* 🔑	reunion *(n.)*

🔑 Oxford 5000™ words   OPAL Oxford Phrasal Academic Lexicon

iQ PRACTICE Go online to listen and practice your pronunciation.
Practice > Unit 7 > Activity 7

WORK WITH THE LISTENING

🔊 **A. LISTEN AND TAKE NOTES** List the important details you hear in the report. Do not try to write complete sentences. Instead, write down only the important words.

B. CATEGORIZE Use your notes to complete the timeline. Choose the events you think are most important. Then compare your answers with a partner.

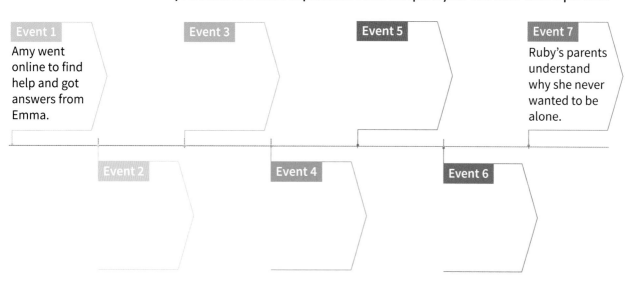

Event 1
Amy went online to find help and got answers from Emma.

Event 2

Event 3

Event 4

Event 5

Event 6

Event 7
Ruby's parents understand why she never wanted to be alone.

🔊 **C. EXPLAIN** Listen again. Then answer the questions.

1. How did Emma Smith and Amy White first get to know each other?

_____

_____

2. Why was Kate's mother, Amy, shocked when she saw the photograph of Ruby?

_____

_____

3. How did Ruby and Kate get along when they saw each other for the second time at a reunion?

_____

_____

4. Why did the parents decide to have a DNA test performed?

_____

_____

5. What did the DNA test results show?

_____

_____

6. How did Ruby react to the test results?

_____

_____

D. IDENTIFY Read the questions. Circle the correct answers.

1. Where were Ruby and Kate born?

   a. They were born in Florida.

   b. They were born in China.

2. How did Ruby behave when she first went to live with her adoptive parents?

   a. She cried a lot.

   b. She slept a lot.

3. How did Kate behave when she went to live with her new parents?

   a. She ate a lot.

   b. She cried a lot.

4. What advice did Emma Smith give Amy about dealing with Kate's eating problem?

   a. She suggested that they share a plate in the middle of the table.

   b. She suggested that they let Kate eat as much as she wanted.

5. Why did Emma and Amy exchange photographs of their daughters?

   a. They noticed that their daughters shared the same date of birth.

   b. They noticed that their daughters were from the same orphanage.

6. What reason does Kate give for why she and Ruby would like to live next door to each other?

   a. They want to go to the same school.

   b. They want to play together.

7. According to Emma Smith, why did Ruby never want to be alone?

   a. She was scared of her new parents.

   b. She had never been alone, even before she was born.

E. DISCUSS Work in a group to discuss the questions.

1. Do you think it is a good idea to encourage the relationship between the two sisters? If so, do you think these families are doing enough to help the sisters?

2. According to the mothers, the girls seemed to "remember" each other and have a natural bond. How would you explain the girls' immediate relationship?

F. VOCABULARY Here are some words from Listening 2. Complete each sentence with the correct word.

ache (v.)	biological (adj.)	in all probability (adv. phr.)
adopt (v.)	deprived (adj.)	odds (n.)
alert (adj.)	face to face (adv. phr.)	reunion (n.)

1. Amy and Ed have one son. Next year they want to _____ another baby boy. Then they will have two sons.

2. I'm looking forward to our class _____. I haven't seen my classmates in so many years!

3. Derek is usually late to class. _____, he'll be late today as well.

4. My brother may be adopted, but I feel like he's my _____ brother.

5. Ever since Lisa was a baby, she has been very _____. She seems to notice everything that happens around her.

6. Eric was in a serious car accident, but the _____ that he will recover completely are very good.

7. I think I'm getting old. Every morning my knees _____, and my back hurts, too.

8. Although we have texted and emailed each other many times, Janet and I have never met _____. I hope I get to meet her someday.

9. Lucas was born in a very poor city and was _____ of many things. He rarely had a home to sleep in.

iQ PRACTICE Go online for more practice with the vocabulary.
Practice > Unit 7 > Activity 8

WORK WITH THE VIDEO

A. PREVIEW What have scientists learned about how the human brain functions?

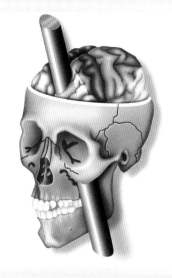

Phineas Gage

iQ RESOURCES Go online to watch the video about how the tragedy of Phineas Gage helped us discover more about the human brain.
Resources > Video > Unit 7 > Unit Video

B. CATEGORIZE Watch the video two or three times. Take notes about the details you hear. Use your notes to make a timeline of the main events in the story.

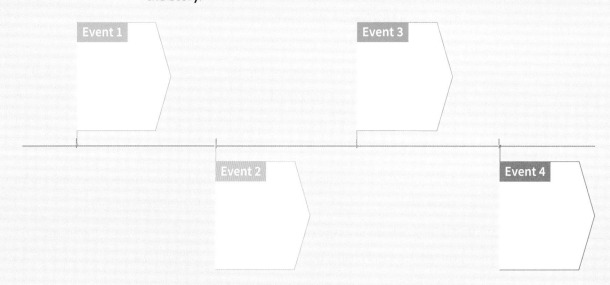

Event 1

Event 3

Event 2

Event 4

C. EXTEND What might be the disadvantages to relying on serendipity to help us understand the human brain?

SAY WHAT YOU THINK

SYNTHESIZE Think about Listening 1, Listening 2, and the unit video as you discuss the questions.

1. Think about the scientific discoveries discussed in the unit video and Listening 1 and the personal discovery from Listening 2. Do you think all of these discoveries were truly accidental? What factors may have helped lead people to these discoveries?

2. Can you think of any ways in which accidental discoveries may have a negative effect on our lives? Discuss any examples you can think of. Consider both scientific discoveries and personal discoveries.

VOCABULARY SKILL Collocations with prepositions

Collocations are combinations of words that are used together frequently. For example, some adjectives and verbs are commonly used with particular prepositions. Part of learning to use these adjectives and verbs correctly involves knowing which prepositions are often used with them.

Here are a few **adjective + preposition** collocations.

embarrassed about	happy about	ready for
fond of	proud of	upset about

Here are a few **verb + preposition** collocations.

complain about	believe in	decide on
arrive at	trip over	approve of

Some collocations are *separable*. A direct object can come between the verb and the preposition.

   bring the twins **together**   **combine** the rubber **with** sulfur

Using common collocations will help you develop your fluency.

A. IDENTIFY Listen to these sentences. Circle the prepositions that you hear.

TIP FOR SUCCESS

Look up verbs and adjectives in a collocations dictionary to find out which prepositions they are commonly used with. It's useful to learn these phrases as you would learn single words.

1. She was looking around, and she was very aware ____ what was going on.

   a. for   b. over   c. of

2. Since it's important ____ Kate, I think it's important to all of us.

   a. at   b. for   c. to

3. Because we hardly ever fight, and we agree ____ a lot of things.

   a. about   b. on   c. in

4. My daughter has not asked me a single question about her birth family or searching ____ them since she's got Kate in her life.

   a. with   b. about   c. for

B. APPLY Read the sentences. Complete each sentence with a collocation from the box.

afraid of	stumbling over
filled ____ with	mixed ____ with

1. The idea is to have them interact in open play-like environments, to encourage them not to be _____ failure, and to build together.

2. Serendipity refers to looking for one thing and _____ something else.

3. Rubber was an unreliable, smelly mess until Charles Goodyear _____ it _____ sulfur.

4. Nomads _____ bags _____ milk and hung them from their saddles as they rode camels.

iQ PRACTICE Go online for more practice using collocations with prepositions. *Practice > Unit 7 > Activity 9*

SPEAKING

OBJECTIVE ▶

At the end of this unit, you are going to tell a personal story about an accidental discovery you made and how it affected you. As you tell the story, you will need to use questions to maintain listener interest.

GRAMMAR Indirect speech

Direct speech reports what someone said using the speaker's exact words.

☐ The teacher said, "You will have a test on Friday."

Indirect speech also reports what someone said, but without using the speaker's exact words.

☐ The teacher said we would have a test on Friday.

When using indirect speech to report what a speaker said in the past, the verb the speaker used must be changed to a past form.

> **Direct speech:**
> Wells said, "The whole idea **is** to bring together people with vastly different backgrounds."
> **Indirect speech:**
> Wells said the whole idea **was** to bring together people with vastly different backgrounds.

When using indirect speech to report a *yes/no* question, use *if* or *whether*.

> **Direct speech:**
> Kate asked her mother, "Is Ruby from China?"
> **Indirect speech:**
> Kate asked her mother **if** Ruby was from China.

When using indirect speech to report a *wh-* question, use the same *wh-* word as the speaker.

> **Direct speech:**
> He asked the professor, "**When** was the microwave oven developed?"
> **Indirect speech:**
> He asked the professor **when** the microwave oven was developed.

When using indirect speech to report information that is generally true or still true now, it is not necessary to shift the verb to a past form.

> **Direct speech:**
> Kate said, "**It's** fun being with Ruby."
> **Indirect speech:**
> Kate said that **it's** fun being with Ruby.

iQ RESOURCES Go online to watch the Grammar Skill Video.
Resources ＞ Video ＞ Unit 7 ＞ Grammar Skill Video

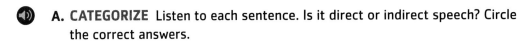

A. CATEGORIZE Listen to each sentence. Is it direct or indirect speech? Circle the correct answers.

1. direct	indirect		5. direct	indirect
2. direct	indirect		6. direct	indirect
3. direct	indirect		7. direct	indirect
4. direct	indirect		8. direct	indirect

B. RESTATE Read these sentences. Rewrite each sentence, changing the direct speech to indirect speech. Then work with a partner to practice saying both versions of each sentence.

1. The professor said, "The discovery of dynamite is an example of serendipity."

_____

2. Mary Tanner said, "My favorite accidental discovery is the invention of Post-it Notes."

_____

3. The professor said, "Dr. Spencer invented something that would revolutionize cooking."

_____

4. The professor said, "We see microwave ovens just about everywhere."

_____

5. Amy said, "I was shocked."

_____

6. Ruby said, "The hole in my heart is getting smaller."

_____

7. Ruby said, "I am Kate," and Kate said, "I am Ruby."

_____

8. In her message, Emma said, "I don't know if my baby knows Amy's baby."

_____

iQ PRACTICE Go online for more practice with indirect speech.
Practice > Unit 7 > Activity 10

iQ PRACTICE Go online for the Grammar Expansion: punctuation in direct and indirect speech. *Practice > Unit 7 > Activity 11*

Speakers often link words together so that the last sound in one word connects to the first sound in the next word. Sometimes it's difficult to tell where one word ends and another word begins.

When words ending with the vowel sounds *-ee, -ey, -ah,* and *-oh* are followed by a word beginning with a vowel, the vowels in the two words link together with the /y/ sound. Because the words are pronounced with no pause between them, it may sound like the second word begins with /y/.

Listen to these sentences and notice how the bold words link with a /y/ sound.

She always wants to **say it**.

Tell me **why it's** important to **be early**.

When words ending with the vowel sounds *-oo, -oh,* and *-ah* are followed by a word beginning with a vowel, the vowels link together with the /w/ sound. Because the words are pronounced with no pause between them, it may sound like the second word begins with /w/.

Listen to these sentences and notice how the bold words link with a /w/ sound.

Can she **go out** with us?

Please **show us** your **new invention**.

Linking words is an important part of fluent pronunciation. Practicing this skill will help to make your speech sound more natural.

 A. APPLY Listen to these pairs of words. Then repeat the words.

1. early age
2. very alert
3. stay awake
4. fly out
5. you opened
6. know about
7. go over
8. how interesting

B. APPLY Listen to these sentences. Draw a line to show where the vowels link together. Write *y* or *w* between the words to show the linking sound. Then practice saying the sentences with a partner.

1. Kate also seemed very deprived, because they noticed she ate as if she'd never eat again.

2. After the fact, serendipity always seems so obvious.

3. Because we hardly ever fight, we agree on a lot of things.

4. Try and spot the next big thing.

5. So after you opened the file, can you recall how it felt?

iQ PRACTICE Go online for more practice with linked words with vowels.
Practice > Unit 7 > Activity 12

When giving a presentation or telling a story, you can keep listeners interested by asking them questions. At the beginning of a presentation, a question can spark interest in your topic. During a presentation, a question can help maintain interest. At the end of your presentation, a question encourages your listeners to keep thinking about your topic after you are done speaking.

There are two main types of questions that speakers ask an audience.

Rhetorical questions are questions that do not require an answer from the audience. Use them to get your listeners to think about what you are about to say.

> What was the most important invention of the twentieth century?
>
> We all might not agree, but today I'd like to talk to you about one very important invention . . .

Interactive questions are questions for which you expect an answer. Use them to interact with your listeners and encourage them to respond to what you are saying.

> **Presenter:** Does anyone know who discovered the law of gravity?
>
> **Audience member:** I think it was Isaac Newton.
>
> **Presenter:** That's right. And the story behind that discovery is an interesting one . . .

Using questions when you present is an effective way to keep the audience paying attention and to help them remember your most important points.

A. EVALUATE Listen to the excerpts from lectures. Which questions are rhetorical and which are interactive? Circle the correct answers.

1. rhetorical   interactive   3. rhetorical   interactive

2. rhetorical   interactive   4. rhetorical   interactive

B. IDENTIFY Listen to this short story about another accidental invention. Then answer the questions.

The Popsicle™

The Popsicle™ is a popular summertime treat in the United States. Kids have been enjoying them for decades. But most people don't know that the Popsicle™ was invented by an 11-year-old.

In 1905, Frank Epperson filled a cup with water and fruit-flavored "soda powder," a mix that was used to make a popular drink. Frank left his drink outside on his porch with a stir stick in it. He forgot all about it and went to bed. That night, the temperature dropped to below freezing in San Francisco, where Frank lived. When he woke up the next morning, he discovered that his fruit drink had frozen to the stir stick. He pulled the frozen mixture out of the cup by the stick, creating a fruit-flavored ice treat.

In 1923, Frank Epperson began making and selling his ice treats in different flavors. By 1928, Frank had sold over 60 million Popsicles™, and his business had made him very wealthy. Nowadays, over three million Popsicles™ are sold each year.

Popsicles™ aren't the only invention made by accident. But they might be the tastiest.

TIP FOR SUCCESS

When asking interactive questions, make sure to give your listeners enough time to answer.

1. Which of these would be the most appropriate rhetorical question to start a presentation about this story?

   a. What is one of the tastiest treats ever invented?

   b. What year did Frank Epperson sell his first Popsicle™?

   c. What is the number of Popsicles™ sold every year?

2. Which of these would be the most appropriate interactive question to ask about how Frank Epperson discovered his frozen treat?

   a. What was Frank's favorite flavor of soda water?

   b. What city did Frank live in?

   c. What do you think Frank found the next morning when he went outside?

3. Which of these would be the most appropriate question to ask at the conclusion of your presentation?

   a. Why did Frank choose the name Popsicle™?

   b. Doesn't a Popsicle™ sound tasty right now?

   c. Which is the most popular flavor?

C. RESTATE In a group, practice telling the story in Activity B in your own words. Use questions to keep your listeners' interest.

iQ PRACTICE Go online for more practice using questions to maintain listener interest. *Practice > Unit 7 > Activity 13*

CRITICAL THINKING STRATEGY

Combining ideas

Putting ideas together in a new way shows you understand material and can think creatively. For instance, on many standardized English exams, you have to combine the ideas in a listening text and a reading text and show how they are connected. Also, when you combine the ideas from your textbook with the ideas shared in a lecture, you will have a deeper understanding of the course materials.

iQ PRACTICE Go online to watch the Critical Thinking Video and check your comprehension. *Practice > Unit 7 > Activity 14*

D. SYNTHESIZE Work with a partner. Read the paragraphs and brainstorm about how the Rosetta Stone and emojis might have the same function. Take notes about how the Rosetta Stone and emojis are similar. Share your ideas with a partner.

The Rosetta Stone	Emojis

In July 1799, two French soldiers discovered a piece of stone with symbols all over it. It eventually helped Egyptologists understand Ancient Egyptian hieroglyphs because it had the same text written in three different ways: hieroglyphics, ancient Greek, and another Ancient Egyptian script.	Emojis are everywhere. Some studies show they are used by up to 90% of the population. Emojis, as I am sure you know, are a pictographic and ideographic writing system that uses symbols to represent an object or idea without using words.

UNIT ASSIGNMENT Tell a story

OBJECTIVE ▶

In this assignment, you are going to tell a personal story about an accidental discovery you made and how it affected you. As you prepare your story, think about the Unit Question, "How can accidental discoveries affect our lives?" Use information from Listening 1, Listening 2, the unit video, and your work in this unit to support your story. Refer to the Self-Assessment checklist on page 176.

CONSIDER THE IDEAS

Look at the list of ideas about discovery. Choose the four ideas you think are the most important factors in making any kind of discovery. Then discuss your answers and reasons with a partner.

desire to succeed	previous experience	tools and resources
fortunate accidents	self-confidence	trying new things
intelligence	supportive people	
making difficult choices	time	

PREPARE AND SPEAK

A. GATHER IDEAS Think about your discussion in the Consider the Ideas activity. Take brief notes on important ideas from your discussion about accidental discoveries. Include reasons that support your ideas.

B. ORGANIZE IDEAS Think of a personal discovery in your life. For example, think about a time when you discovered you had a talent for a sport or a subject in school. If you can't think of a personal discovery, borrow one from someone else's life experience.

1. How do the ideas in your notes from Activity A apply to this discovery?

2. Make notes about the major events involved in the discovery. List them in the order they happened. Say how this discovery affected you.

Personal discovery:

Events	Details

Effect:

C. SPEAK Use your notes to present your story. Remember to explain the steps in how the discovery occurred and how it affected you. As you tell your story, use one or more questions to maintain the interest of your listeners. Refer to the Self-Assessment checklist below before you begin.

iQ PRACTICE Go online for your alternate Unit Assignment.
Practice > Unit 7 > Activity 15

CHECK AND REFLECT

A. CHECK Think about the Unit Assignment as you complete the Self-Assessment checklist.

SELF-ASSESSMENT	Yes	No
I was able to speak easily about the topic.	☐	☐
My partner, group, and class understood me.	☐	☐
I used signal words.	☐	☐
I used vocabulary from the unit.	☐	☐
I used questions to maintain listeners' interest.	☐	☐
I linked words with vowels.	☐	☐

B. REFLECT Discuss these questions with a partner or group.

1. What is something new you learned in this unit?

2. Look back at the Unit Question—How can accidental discoveries affect our lives? Is your answer different now than when you started this unit? If yes, how is it different? Why?

iQ PRACTICE Go to the online discussion board to discuss the questions.
Practice > Unit 7 > Activity 16

TRACK YOUR SUCCESS

iQ PRACTICE Go online to check the words and phrases you have learned in this unit. *Practice > Unit 7 > Activity 17*

Check (✓) the skills and strategies you learned. If you need more work on a skill, refer to the page(s) in parentheses.

LISTENING	☐ I can listen for signal words and phrases. (p. 158)
NOTE-TAKING	☐ I can take notes on details. (p. 160)
VOCABULARY	☐ I can use collocations with prepositions. (p. 167)
GRAMMAR	☐ I can use indirect speech. (p. 169)
PRONUNCIATION	☐ I can link words with vowels. (p. 171)
SPEAKING	☐ I can use questions to maintain listener interest. (p. 172)
CRITICAL THINKING	☐ I can combine ideas from different sources. (p. 174)

OBJECTIVE ▶ ☐ I can gather information and ideas to tell a personal story about an accidental discovery I made and how it affected me.

Engineering

8

What are the consequences of progress?

A. Discuss these questions with your classmates.

1. What are some important inventions of the past 50 years? How did they change people's lives for the better?

2. What are some unintended consequences of recent inventions? What problems that we face now are the result of "progress"?

3. Look at the photo. What technology is shown here? How could this technology be used?

B. Listen to *The Q Classroom* online. Then answer these questions.

1. Sophy and Marcus talk about some problems using smartphones can cause. Can you think of any others?

2. According to Felix, the pros of using smartphones might outweigh the cons. Do you agree? Why or why not?

iQ PRACTICE   Go to the online discussion board to discuss the Unit Question with your classmates. *Practice > Unit 8 > Activity 1*

UNIT OBJECTIVE

Listen to a radio interview and a lecture and gather information and ideas to present your opinions about the consequences of progress.

LISTENING 1 Automation and Us

OBJECTIVE ▶

You are going to listen to a radio interview about automation from the Canadian Broadcasting Corporation. It explores some of the consequences of the use of machines to do work that was previously done by people. As you listen to the interview, gather information and ideas about the consequences of progress.

PREVIEW THE LISTENING

A. PREVIEW What do you think are some consequences of automation? Look at the photos of three different advancements. Make a note about a possible positive consequence and a possible negative consequence. Then discuss your answers with a partner.

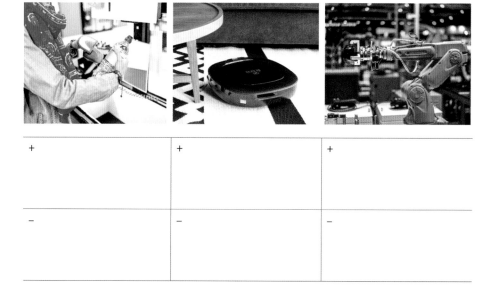

+	+	+
–	–	–

B. VOCABULARY Read aloud these words from Listening 1. Check (✓) the ones you know. Use a dictionary to define any new or unknown words. Then discuss with a partner how the words will relate to the unit.

dependency *(n.)*	generic *(adj.)* 🔑	necessarily *(adv.)* 🔑 OPAL
diversity *(n.)* 🔑 OPAL	idle *(adj.)*	philosophical *(adj.)* 🔑
engagement *(n.)* 🔑	intimate *(adj.)* 🔑	subtle *(adj.)* 🔑
fulfilled *(adj.)*	manual *(adj.)*	uniformity *(n.)*

🔑 Oxford 5000™ words   OPAL Oxford Phrasal Academic Lexicon

iQ PRACTICE Go online to listen and practice your pronunciation.
Practice > Unit 8 > Activity 2

WORK WITH THE LISTENING

A. LISTEN AND TAKE NOTES Listen to the radio interview and use the chart below to take notes on the unexpected effects of automation.

iQ RESOURCES Go online to download extra vocabulary support.
Resources > Extra Vocabulary > Unit 8

Type of automation	Expected effects	Unexpected effects
medical record-keeping	- doctors would become more efficient	- -
automatic pilot systems	- flying would become safer	-

B. EXTEND Work with a partner. Use your notes to summarize the consequences of automation. Did any surprise you? Explain why.

C. IDENTIFY Match each cause with its effect.

_____ 1. People are working.

_____ 2. Doctors bring tablets into exam rooms.

_____ 3. Much of our work involves data entry and looking at screens.

_____ 4. Automated systems are used to fly airplanes.

_____ 5. Pilots fall out of practice manually operating an airplane.

a. People are doing less diverse and creative work.

b. People are generally safer.

c. People get more unnecessary medical tests.

d. People are in danger when automatic systems fail.

e. People are happier and more fulfilled.

D. IDENTIFY Listen to the radio interview again. Circle the answer that best completes each statement.

1. According to Nicholas Carr, people tend to feel more satisfied if they are working because ____.

   a. they make money to support their families

   b. they can use their talents to overcome challenges

   c. they can use automation to make their jobs easier

2. People assumed that automation would allow doctors to ____.

   a. share information more easily

   b. see more patients in a day

   c. order more unnecessary tests

3. Tablets and computers are actually causing a lack of intimacy between doctors and patients because ____.

   a. doctors are assuming that patients need more tests than they actually do

   b. doctors are busier entering data into a computer, and they don't have time to talk to their patients

   c. doctors aren't making eye contact with their patients as much during a visit

4. According to Nicholas Carr, when we do more of our work using automation, our work becomes ____.

   a. more uniform and less interesting

   b. more diverse and skillful

   c. more satisfying

5. Because automation has taken over the physical job of a pilot, ____.

    a. pilots are free to concentrate on flying the plane more safely

    b. pilots manually fly the plane for about three minutes every flight

    c. pilots have totally forgotten how to respond in an emergency

E. IDENTIFY Read the statements. Check (✓) the opinions that Nicholas Carr would probably agree with. Then compare your answers with a partner and explain your choices.

☐ 1. "This concern about automation is a little exaggerated. Unless you work in a factory, you are not going to lose your job to a robot."

☐ 2. "Automation is the future, whether we like it or not. We need to learn how to develop automation that complements what humans are already good at."

☐ 3. "Increased automation in the workforce is most certainly going to result in an increased demand for creativity. Robots can do the boring work, and we'll do the fun, imaginative work."

☐ 4. "One of the dangers we need to think about as automation becomes the norm for many of us is that it may cause humans to become lazy. We might lose the ability to perform important skills."

☐ 5. "Government or industry leaders need to start thinking about a strategic way forward so that the decisions we make about automation aren't guided by what technology can do for us but by what it should do for us."

F. VOCABULARY Here are some words from Listening 1. Read the sentences. Then write the number of each bold word next to the correct definition.

1. As we grow up, our **dependency** on our parents decreases.

2. Rainforests are important because they are home to a great deal of plant and animal **diversity**.

3. I made my children leave their smartphones at home for a whole day with the family. When they bring them, I see less **engagement** between them.

4. I'm really **fulfilled** in my current job. I have no interest in applying for a different position.

5. As an artist, his goal is to produce unique, creative pieces. He does not want his art to feel **generic** and unoriginal.

6. I took three weeks of vacation over the summer. It felt wonderful to just be **idle** and not rushing around.

7. It's important that doctors develop an **intimate** relationship with their patients so they are comfortable discussing personal health matters.

8. I went to college so I could avoid doing **manual** labor.

9. The number of tickets is **necessarily** limited due to the size of the theater.

10. We were having a **philosophical** debate about good and evil.

11. He gave **subtle** hints about what gift he wanted for his birthday, but even though he wasn't direct, I could still guess.

12. In the suburbs, there is often a **uniformity** to the houses so that many in a neighborhood will look the same.

____ a. (*adj.*) shared by, including, or typical of a whole group of things; not specific

____ b. (*adj.*) involving using the hands or physical strength

____ c. (*adj.*) feeling happy and satisfied that you are doing something useful with your life

____ d. (*adv.*) used to say that something cannot be avoided

____ e. (*n.*) the fact of not varying and of being the same in all parts and at all times

____ f. (*n.*) a range of many people or things that are very different from each other

____ g. (*adj.*) not working hard

____ h. (*adj.*) connected with philosophy

____ i. (*n.*) the state of relying on somebody/something for something

____ j. (*adj.*) having a close and friendly relationship

_____ k. (*n.*) being involved with somebody/something in an attempt to understand them/it

_____ l. (*adj.*) not very noticeable or obvious

iQ PRACTICE Go online for more practice with the vocabulary.
Practice > Unit 8 > Activity 3

iQ PRACTICE Go online for additional listening and comprehension.
Practice > Unit 8 > Activity 4

SAY WHAT YOU THINK

DISCUSS Work in a group to discuss the questions.

1. Would you prefer to see a doctor who uses an automated system to store your medical records or one who uses paper files? Why?

2. What are some solutions to the problems described in Listening 1? Should governments set a policy limiting the development of automation? Should customers complain?

LISTENING SKILL Listening for causes and effects

A speaker may talk about what **causes** something to happen or what **happens because of** some other action or event. Speakers usually use **signal words** that connect two events or ideas.

These are some of the signal words that speakers use to show a **cause**.
because (of)   as a result of   due to   since   by

> **Due to** our belief that we don't like to work, we might think we want to be free from labor.
> **Because** doctors bring tablets into the exam room, they are less connected with their patients.
> **Since** we are trading deep engagement with the world for interaction with computers, we might be less satisfied with our work.

These are some of the signal words that speakers use to show a **result**.
because of this / that   as a result   therefore   so   the result is

> A lot of our time is spent looking at screens. **The result is** uniformity in activities, skills, and talent.
> Doctors now are not as connected with their patients, **so** they may miss important information they would have noticed before.
> Architects and lawyers are finding their work is increasingly involving data entry; **therefore**, they are engaging with the world differently than before.

Knowing these words and phrases will help you understand how the information is organized and predict what a speaker will say next.

ACADEMIC LANGUAGE

There are several other phrases we use to signal causes and effects in speech:

the effect(s) of
what happens if
what happens to
one of the reasons
the reason for
the reason why
so that
to see how

As you speak, try to use different phrases to introduce causes and effects so your speech is interesting and varied.

iQ RESOURCES Go online to watch the Listening Skill Video.
Resources ⟩ Video ⟩ Unit 8 ⟩ Listening Skill Video

A. IDENTIFY Listen to the sentences. Circle the word or phrase you hear in each sentence.

Sentence 1

a. as a result of   b. the result is

Sentence 2

a. therefore   b. because of this

Sentence 3

a. because of   b. due to

Sentence 4

a. as a result   b. the result is

Sentence 5

a. therefore   b. because

Sentence 6

a. since   b. now that

B. CATEGORIZE Read each sentence. Is the underlined section the *cause* or the *effect*? Write *C* (cause) or *E* (effect).

TIP FOR SUCCESS

When listening to a presentation that mentions causes and effects, mark each cause or effect in your notes. Label them with a *C* or an *E*. This will help you make important connections when you review.

_____ 1. Since <u>automation often allows companies to lower costs</u>, we can expect to see lower prices as well.

_____ 2. Due to increased automation, <u>travel agents have experienced employment declines</u>.

_____ 3. People are concerned about losing good jobs to automation, so <u>they argue that it should be limited to dirty or dangerous jobs</u>.

_____ 4. Other people are worried that automation could cause worldwide unemployment. Therefore, <u>they are calling for universal basic income, where the government pays all adults whether they are working or not</u>.

_____ 5. Despite these fears, we need to remember that economic growth could be negatively affected as a result of <u>limits placed on automation</u>.

_____ 6. Since <u>it looks like automation developments are here to stay</u>, we need to do more to help workers transition from threatened jobs into new jobs.

iQ PRACTICE Go online for more practice listening for causes and effects.
Practice ⟩ Unit 8 ⟩ Activity 5

When you are listening to a report, a lecture, an interview, or any kind of presentation that deals with causes and effects, list the causes and effects separately. One way to do this is by using a T-chart. Write causes on one side of the chart and effects on the other side. This will help you understand how the causes and effects relate to each other, and it will make reviewing your notes easier.

A. IDENTIFY Listen and read this section of a lecture on the benefits of digital cameras. Circle the words and phrases that introduce the causes. Underline the words and phrases that introduce effects.

Digital camera technology has made it possible for just about anyone anywhere to take pictures of anything. When you take a picture, the camera captures light rays that enter through the lens. Engineers invented an image sensor chip. When light hits the chip, it basically turns the light rays into a long number. Because of this, they have been able to put digital cameras into our smartphones. Since smartphones are available to almost everyone, it means that everyone can take pictures whenever they have their phones. Also, because digital images are essentially numbers, the pictures we take are easy to edit. We don't need to hire professional photographers as often because we can do the work ourselves for free. So, these days, regular people can take pictures of everything from their meals to events of political or historical importance. While this has resulted in some very silly pictures on the Internet, it has also meant that we can find out about current events more quickly because we are all "journalists" now. The consequences of this change are yet to be determined.

B. CATEGORIZE Complete the student's notes by writing down the missing causes and effects. Listen again if needed.

Causes	Effects
engineers invented _____	- cameras put into smartphones
smartphones are everywhere	- _____
digital pictures = _____	- _____
	- we don't hire photographers as often
people everywhere can take pictures	- _____
	- _____

iQ PRACTICE   Go online for more practice taking notes on causes and effects. *Practice* > *Unit 8* > *Activity 6*

LISTENING 2   Driverless Cars

OBJECTIVE ▶

You are going to listen to a lecture in an engineering class. As you listen, gather information and ideas about the consequences of progress.

PREVIEW THE LISTENING

A. PREVIEW This lecture is about driverless cars. How much do you know about them? How comfortable would you be riding in one? Discuss with a partner.

B. VOCABULARY Read aloud these words from Listening 2. Check (✓) the ones you know. Use a dictionary to define any new or unknown words. Then discuss with a partner how the words will relate to the unit.

abstract *(adj.)* 🍗	gut *(n.)* 🍗	outcome *(n.)* 🍗 OPAL
cater to *(v. phr.)*	harm *(n.)* 🍗 OPAL	prospective *(adj.)* 🍗
dive into *(v. phr.)*	loosely *(adv.)*	theoretically *(adv.)* OPAL
entirely *(adv.)* 🍗 OPAL	notion *(n.)* 🍗 OPAL	

🍗 Oxford 5000™ words OPAL Oxford Phrasal Academic Lexicon

iQ PRACTICE Go online to listen and practice your pronunciation.
Practice > Unit 8 > Activity 7

WORK WITH THE LISTENING

A. LISTEN AND TAKE NOTES Listen to the lecture and complete the chart. Then compare your chart with a partner.

iQ RESOURCES Go online to download extra vocabulary support.
Resources > Extra Vocabulary > Unit 8

Causes	Effects
Workers not driving	
People not behind the wheel	
Cars can be programmed to do least harm in an accident	

B. IDENTIFY Read the sentences. Circle the answer that best completes each statement.

1. Some experts are predicting that, because of driverless cars, ____.

   a. millions of jobs will disappear

   b. more accidents will happen

   c. cars will still look the same

2. We may not need to buy insurance because driverless cars will ____.

   a. never crash

   b. be completely safe

   c. never make human errors

3. Our notion of what a car looks like will change ____.

   a. based on insurance companies' rules

   b. to provide us with things to do while on the road

   c. as a result of changes in the economy

4. When they are asked, most people say that cars should be programmed to ____.

   a. make decisions that do the least harm

   b. protect the weakest members of society

   c. make the same decisions that a human would make

5. When people were asked who a driverless car should protect if they were passengers, they said ____.

   a. the car should always protect the youngest, healthiest pedestrian

   b. they wanted the car to be programmed to do the least harm

   c. they wouldn't buy a car that didn't protect the passenger

6. Self-driving cars are an example of technological progress ____.

   a. with unintended consequences

   b. that causes many problems

   c. making life better for everyone

C. **APPLY** Listen again. Complete these sentences.

1. As a result of the invention of driverless cars, truck stops

   _____ .

2. Because of driverless cars, car designers

   _____ .

3. Due to the creation of movie cars and spa cars,

   _____ .

4. People don't want to buy a car that wouldn't protect them, so

   _____ .

5. Overall, driverless cars will reduce the number of accidents. Because of this,

   _____ .

D. **DISCUSS** Work in a small group to discuss the questions.

1. Who should be responsible for helping people who lose their jobs as driverless cars become more common? Should the government help them find new employment? How?

2. If you were a designer of a driverless car, what special features would you include in your design to make traveling more comfortable and enjoyable for passengers?

3. How do you feel about cars having the power to make life-or-death decisions? What are some advantages and disadvantages of this?

4. Some people predict that car ownership will decline and people will order driverless cars to take them places rather than pay to buy and maintain a personal vehicle. Would you prefer to order or own a car?

E. VOCABULARY Here are some words from Listening 2. Complete each sentence with the correct word.

abstract *(adj.)*	cater to *(v. phr.)*	dive into *(v. phr.)*	entirely *(adv.)*
gut *(n.)*	harm *(n.)*	loosely *(adv.)*	notion *(n.)*
outcome *(n.)*	prospective *(adj.)*	theoretically *(adv.)*	

1. It's easy to understand the meaning of new English words when you can see a photo, but understanding _____ vocabulary can be more difficult.

2. When you work in a kitchen, you have to be careful not to _____ yourself with anything very hot or sharp.

3. When I take on a new project, I just _____ the work.

4. I'm not sure if it will work, but _____ the plans make sense.

5. Children's stores usually _____ a younger customer.

6. The movie is _____ based on the novel. The plot is similar, but there are some pretty big differences.

7. When he met her, he knew in his _____ that she was the right person for him to spend the rest of his life with.

8. The contest is really close, and people are very curious about the _____.

9. I really wasn't sure what the class was about. I only had the _____ that we would be learning about philosophy.

10. She spent the day showing the house to _____ buyers, but no one made an offer to buy it.

11. Their menu was almost _____ made up of pizza and pasta. There weren't many other options.

iQ PRACTICE Go online for more practice with the vocabulary.
Practice › Unit 8 › Activity 8

CRITICAL THINKING STRATEGY

Making appraisals

In Unit 5, you learned about evaluating information. Evaluating information allows you to make appraisals. When we read or listen to information, we may need to give a value to the information or the topic of the text based on the facts and opinions the text contains. When you come across new information, you need to think about where it is coming from and use your background knowledge to judge if the claims seem reasonable. Then you can use your evaluation of the information to decide how much of your money, time, or energy something is worth. This demonstrates a deeper understanding of the material and allows us to make informed decisions about information we receive.

iQ PRACTICE Go online to watch the Critical Thinking Video and check your comprehension. *Practice > Unit 8 > Activity 9*

F. **IDENTIFY** Look at the advertisements. Make an appraisal of the products they describe. For each product, decide whether you would be willing to pay the average price, a lower price, or a higher price. Discuss your answers with a partner.

"Nine out of ten dentists agree that Toothy Toothpaste is the most effective toothpaste on the market for preventing cavities."

"Engineers believe the Wave is the safest car available to consumers, and the Wave is the winner of three national safety awards."

"Researchers agree that the future of weight loss is the Weight Loss Winner pill. Just one pill a day melts the fat away."

G. DISCUSS Work with a partner. Answer the questions about each advertisement.

1. Where is the information coming from? Can you believe the "experts"? Why or why not?

2. Think about what you know about life and what you learned in school. Does the information in each advertisement seem possible? Why or why not?

WORK WITH THE VIDEO

A. PREVIEW In some places, driverless trucks are already being used. Look at the picture below. How would you feel if you were sitting in the passenger seat of a driverless semitrailer truck? What concerns would you have?

VIDEO VOCABULARY

disrupt *(v.)* to make it difficult for something to continue in the normal way

freight *(n.)* goods that are transported by ships, planes, trains, or trucks

pedal *(n.)* a part of a bicycle, car, etc., that you push or press with your foot to make the machine move or work

from scratch *(idm.)* from the very beginning, not using any of the work done before

traitor *(n.)* a person who works against their friends, country, etc.

remotely *(adv.)* from a distance

autonomously *(adv.)* with the ability to work without any help from anyone

iQ RESOURCES Go online to watch the video about new technology that may soon make many trucks driverless. *Resources > Video > Unit 8 > Unit Video*

B. IDENTIFY Watch the video two or three times. Take notes about the effects that driverless technology could have on the world.

Causes	Effects
Stefan and his team are adapting existing trucks.	
Stefan and his team added a computer to control a truck's pedals and steering wheel.	
Stefan's type of self-driving truck will still require drivers.	
Stefan and his team are focusing specifically on highway driving.	

C. DISCUSS Read the quotation from the speaker in this video and answer the questions. Discuss with a partner.

"Once you're out there doing it and you're dealing with real-life problems, things going slightly wrong, fixing them up, you can then demonstrate to the world that we have made this thing work. We're not going to wait around for all the regulations. And then almost by virtue of demonstrating its power, it forces the world to change around it."

1. Do you think this is a good way to cause change?

2. What are some of the potential consequences of changes that come too quickly?

SAY WHAT YOU THINK

SYNTHESIZE Think about Listening 1, Listening 2, and the unit video as you discuss the questions.

1. In general, does making progress usually have positive or negative consequences? What examples can you think of to support your opinion?

2. Whose job should it be to regulate progress? An international agency, like the United Nations? The government in each country? Businesses? Scientists and engineers?

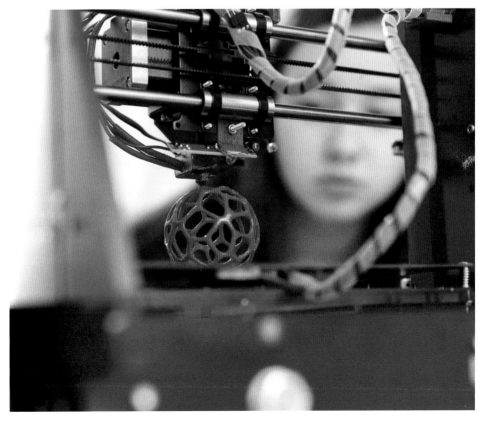

An **idiom** is a particular group of words that has a specific meaning different from the individual words in it. Idioms function as a separate unit, almost as if they were a single word.

On the other hand means "in contrast."

⌐ But **on the other hand**, isn't flying, for instance, safer than ever before, thanks to
  automation?

Fall victim to means "to be negatively affected by something."

⌐ Pilots often **fall victim to** what researchers call "automation complacency."

Because idioms have specific meanings, much like individual words do, it is useful to remember these "chunks" of language in the same way you memorize individual words.

There are thousands of idioms. Most of these idioms are not in the dictionary. For this reason, it is important that you notice them when they occur and use context clues to figure out their meaning.

🔊 **A. IDENTIFY** Listen to the excerpts from Listening 1 and Listening 2. Listen for each idiom and how it is used. Then match each idiom with its definition in the box.

TIP FOR SUCCESS

Idioms can be difficult to understand, especially in conversation. When someone uses an idiom you are not familiar with, use a clarification strategy. You can also use context to understand the meaning, and some idioms can be found in a collocations dictionary.

a. something to worry about

b. remember

c. not as good as it used to be because you have not been practicing

d. at risk

e. with no particular activities; free

_____ 1. at leisure

_____ 2. rusty

_____ 3. cause for concern

_____ 4. on the line

_____ 5. keep in mind

B. COMPOSE Create sentences using the five idioms in Activity A. Practice saying the sentences with a partner.

iQ PRACTICE   Go online for more practice using idioms.
Practice > Unit 8 > Activity 10

SPEAKING

OBJECTIVE ▶

At the end of this unit, you are going share your opinions about the consequences of progress. As you speak, you will need to add to other speakers' comments.

GRAMMAR Real conditionals

Real conditional sentences show a possible or expected cause and effect. They can give information about the present or the future.

Most real conditionals have a conditional clause containing *if* and a simple present verb connected to a main clause with a simple present or future verb.

> conditional clause   main clause
>
> If driverless cars **become** popular, people **will** lose their jobs.
> (People will lose their jobs as a result of driverless cars becoming popular.)

Conditional clauses can also begin with *when* or *whenever* to describe a general truth or habit.

> conditional clause   main clause
>
> When a doctor **has** a computer, the doctor **will order** more diagnostic tests.
> (Doctors order more tests as a result of having a computer.)

The conditional clause can come before or after the main clause. If the conditional clause comes first, there is a pause, shown by a comma, between the clauses.

> If you don't have to drive, how do you spend your time?
> How do you spend your time if you don't have to drive?

Real conditionals can be used to express many kinds of ideas.

Things that will become true

☐ If he can find old wood, Rick will make a guitar.

Predictions

☐ If we don't have to drive cars anymore, how they look will change.

Habits

☐ When doctors bring their computers into an exam room, they order more tests.

Deals, compromises, and promises

☐ "I'll make Bob Dylan a guitar from Chumley's wood if he asks."

Advice

☐ If you rely too much on automation, do a couple of things manually each day.

Warnings

☐ When pilots don't get enough manual practice, they make mistakes in
  emergency situations.

Instructions

☐ When you see someone throwing away old wood, grab it from them.

A. **APPLY** Read the sentences. Rewrite or restate each one so that the conditional clause comes first. Then practice saying the sentences with a partner.

1. More automation is not necessarily good when it isn't designed to benefit humans.

2. We can require pilots to practice flying manually if we are worried about their skills getting rusty.

3. You should think about getting into a different industry if you are worried about a robot replacing you.

4. I don't like getting more medical tests when I don't need them.

5. I'll buy an exercise car when they are invented.

6. They'll redesign cars when they all become driverless.

7. You can't be sure of people's answers if you don't ask them the question.

8. Automation advancements are certain if things continue as we expect.

B. **COMPOSE** For each situation, write a conditional sentence using the type of conditional in parentheses. Then compare answers with a partner.

1. A car company wants to sell a driverless car that is programmed to protect pedestrians in case of an emergency. (warning)

2. Your friend just bought a driverless car. You'd like a ride. In exchange, you can offer to pay for the gas. (deal)

3. You believe that computers in cars will be able to communicate with each other in the next couple of years. (prediction)

4. Your friend is a journalist. She is worried about her job being taken by a computer programmed to write news stories. (advice)

iQ PRACTICE   Go online for more practice with real conditionals.
Practice > Unit 8 > Activity 11

iQ PRACTICE   Go online for the Grammar Expansion: review of real and unreal conditionals. *Practice > Unit 8 > Activity 12*

PRONUNCIATION Thought groups

Speakers don't talk in a steady, continuous stream of words. Instead, they say their words as **thought groups** to help listeners understand their ideas. Speakers separate thought groups with brief pauses.

A thought group may be a short sentence.

Automation isn't always a good thing.

                thought group

It may be part of a longer sentence.

      I'm not worried   that robots will take over the planet.

      thought group 1   thought group 2

  However, I think my father is suspicious about his new virtual assistant.

thought group 1   thought group 2   thought group 3

It may be a word, a short phrase, or a clause. The end of a sentence is always the end of the thought group.

      Ultimately, we usually like technology that makes life easier.

    thought group 1   thought group 2   thought group 3

When speaking, think about how to form your ideas into thought groups to help your listeners understand your ideas.

A. IDENTIFY Listen to the speaker. Draw slashes (/) between the thought groups.

people always ask me what advice do you have for workers who are facing an increasingly automated workplace first get a college education experts agree that blue-collar jobs will be most in danger second focus on working in a job that machines and robots haven't proven very good at such as working with customers being creative planning managing people or directing finally if it looks like the writing is on the wall for your particular field of expertise be flexible consider transitioning to other work

B. APPLY Practice reading the sentences in Activity A with a partner. Focus on separating thought groups.

iQ PRACTICE   Go online for more practice with thought groups.
Practice > Unit 8 > Activity 13

SPEAKING SKILL Adding to another speaker's comments

One way to keep a conversation interesting is **to build on someone else's ideas**. Sometimes you want to communicate that you agree with another speaker or add other ideas related to the topic.

These phrases can be used to add to the conversation.

To show agreement	To build on an idea
I agree	Plus . . .
That's a good point	Furthermore . . .
That's true	I would add that . . .
Right	Another important point is (that) . . .
Exactly	To build on what you said . . .
	Going back to what you before . . .

Phrases of agreement can be combined with phrases that build on an idea.

I agree. I would also add (that) . . .
Exactly. I would also add (that) . . .

Listen to the conversation.

Sung-ju: So, while I really enjoy using social media to keep in touch with friends and family, it's a bit creepy when the site automatically labels or tags my photos. I am all for intelligent machines, but I'm not sure I like the idea of my computer watching and remembering what I do.

David: <u>That's true! Plus,</u> I hate when social networking sites push advertisements that they think I'm interested in.

A. IDENTIFY Listen to a discussion about potential consequences of a common form of automation. Check (✓) the phrases of agreement and the building phrases you hear. Then work with a partner to summarize the main points.

☐ Another important point is that . . . ☐ That's a good point.

☐ And to build on what John said earlier . . . ☐ Exactly!

☐ Going back to what John said, . . . ☐ I would add that . . .

B. EXTEND Create a list of at least four consequences of using voice recognition.

C. DISCUSS Work in a group. Discuss the reasons you listed in Activity B. Agree with or add to the ideas you hear.

iQ PRACTICE Go online for more practice adding to another speaker's comments. *Practice > Unit 8 > Activity 14*

Share opinions about the consequences of progress

In this assignment, you are going share your opinions about the consequences of progress—both good and bad. As you prepare to share your opinions, think about the Unit Question, "What are the consequences of progress?" Use information from Listening 1, Listening 2, the unit video, and your work in this unit to support your opinions. Refer to the Self-Assessment checklist on page 202.

CONSIDER THE IDEAS

DISCUSS Work with a partner. Discuss the questions about technology and growing older.

1. What challenges do people face as they grow older?

2. What technological advancements have made life easier for elderly people?

3. What challenges do some older people have with technology? How will future products need to be adapted to be useful to older users?

4. Are there any possible negative consequences associated with older people using technology to improve their lifestyles?

PREPARE AND SPEAK

TIP FOR SUCCESS

When participating in a group discussion, write down ideas that you think of while others are speaking. This will help you to remember your ideas when you have an opportunity to take a turn.

A. GATHER IDEAS Look at the photos of technological advancements designed to improve the lives of elderly people. List two potential positive consequences and two potential negative consequences.

Robotic pet	Personal assistant	Medical caregiver
+	+	+
+	+	+
-	-	-
-	-	-

B. ORGANIZE IDEAS Work with a partner. Compare the positive and negative consequences you listed for each product in Activity A. Add to the chart.

C. SPEAK Work in a small group. Follow these steps. Refer to the Self-Assessment checklist below before you begin.

1. Conduct a group discussion on this topic: What are the consequences of elderly people using technology designed to improve their lives?

2. Take turns expressing your ideas. Try to use conditional sentences to express your ideas. Also try to use some of the phrases you learned to add to other speakers' comments. As you speak, use pauses to separate your thought groups.

3. As a group, try to reach a consensus about the most useful (and least potentially harmful) product. Which do you think you would most appreciate when you get older?

iQ PRACTICE Go online for your alternate Unit Assignment.
Practice > Unit 8 > Activity 15

CHECK AND REFLECT

CHECK Think about the Unit Assignment as you complete the Self-Assessment checklist.

SELF-ASSESSMENT	Yes	No
I was able to speak easily about the topic.	☐	☐
I took notes on causes and effects.	☐	☐
My partner, group, and class understood me.	☐	☐
I made appraisals.	☐	☐
I used real conditional sentences.	☐	☐
I used vocabulary from the unit.	☐	☐
I added to other speakers' comments.	☐	☐
I used thought groups while speaking.	☐	☐

D. REFLECT Discuss these questions with a partner or group.

1. What is something new you learned in this unit?

2. Look back at the Unit Question—What are the consequences of progress? Is your answer different now than when you started the unit? If yes, how is it different? Why?

iQ PRACTICE Go to the online discussion board to discuss the questions.
Practice > Unit 8 > Activity 16

TRACK YOUR SUCCESS

iQ PRACTICE Go online to check the words and phrases you have learned in this unit. *Practice ⟩ Unit 8 ⟩ Activity 17*

Check (✓) the skills and strategies you learned. If you need more work on a skill, refer to the page(s) in parentheses.

LISTENING	☐ I can listen for causes and effects. (p. 185)
NOTE-TAKING	☐ I can take notes on causes and effects. (p. 187)
CRITICAL THINKING	☐ I can make appraisals. (p. 193)
VOCABULARY	☐ I can understand idioms. (p. 196)
GRAMMAR	☐ I can use real conditional sentences. (p. 197)
PRONUNCIATION	☐ I can recognize and use thought groups. (p. 199)
SPEAKING	☐ I can add to another speaker's comments. (p. 200)
OBJECTIVE ▶	☐ I can gather information and ideas to share my opinions about the consequences of progress.

VOCABULARY LIST AND CEFR CORRELATION

🔑 The **Oxford 5000**™ is an expanded core word list for advanced learners of English. The words have been chosen based on their frequency in the Oxford English Corpus and relevance to learners of English. As well as the **Oxford 3000**™ core word list, the Oxford 5000 includes an additional 2,000 words that are aligned to the CEFR, guiding advanced learners at B2–C1 level on the most useful high-level words to learn to expand their vocabulary.

OPAL The **Oxford Phrasal Academic Lexicon** is an essential guide to the most important words and phrases to know for academic English. The word lists are based on the Oxford Corpus of Academic English and the British Academic Spoken English corpus.

The **Common European Framework of Reference for Language (CEFR)** provides a basic description of what language learners have to do to use language effectively. The system contains 6 reference levels: A1, A2, B1, B2, C1, C2.

UNIT 1

advance *(v.)* 🔑 B2
assess *(v.)* 🔑 OPAL B2
capable *(adj.)* 🔑 OPAL B2
clarity *(n.)* 🔑 C1
contact *(n.)* 🔑 OPAL B1
effective *(adj.)* 🔑 OPAL B1
enthusiasm *(n.)* 🔑 B2
ethical *(adj.)* 🔑 OPAL B2
executive *(n.)* 🔑 B2
initiative *(n.)* 🔑 OPAL B2
innovation *(n.)* 🔑 B2
motivation *(n.)* 🔑 OPAL B2
perspective *(n.)* 🔑 OPAL B2
promote *(v.)* 🔑 OPAL B1
realistic *(adj.)* 🔑 B2
responsibility *(n.)* 🔑 OPAL B1
role *(n.)* 🔑 OPAL A2
style *(n.)* 🔑 OPAL A1
take on *(v. phr.)* 🔑 B1
title *(n.)* 🔑 OPAL A1
versus *(prep.)* 🔑 OPAL C1

UNIT 2

bias *(n.)* 🔑 OPAL B2
chaos *(n.)* 🔑 C1
embrace *(v.)* 🔑 B2
feature *(n.)* 🔑 OPAL A2
grant *(v.)* 🔑 B2
imply *(v.)* 🔑 OPAL B2

inflexible *(adj.)* C1
legal *(adj.)* 🔑 OPAL B1
manufacture *(v.)* 🔑 B2
moderately *(adv.)* C1
monopoly *(n.)* 🔑 C1
obtain *(v.)* 🔑 OPAL B2
open-minded *(adj.)* C1
point out *(v. phr.)* 🔑 B1
purchase *(n.)* 🔑 B2
recognize *(v.)* 🔑 OPAL A2
revert *(v.)* C2
shade *(n.)* 🔑 B2
stifle *(v.)* C1
stimulating *(adj.)* B2
stumble upon *(v. phr.)* C2
theme *(n.)* 🔑 OPAL B1
trademark *(v.)* 🔑 C1
turn out *(v. phr.)* 🔑 B1

UNIT 3

agency *(n.)* 🔑 B2
asset *(n.)* 🔑 B2
balance *(v.)* 🔑 OPAL B1
current *(adj.)* 🔑 OPAL B1
debt *(n.)* 🔑 B2
entrepreneur *(n.)* 🔑 B2
insurance *(n.)* 🔑 B2
interest *(n.)* 🔑 OPAL A1
minor *(adj.)* 🔑 OPAL B2
mortgage *(n.)* 🔑 B2

naturally *(adv.)* 🔑 OPAL B1
nutrition *(n.)* 🔑 B2
pension *(n.)* 🔑 B2
precisely *(adv.)* 🔑 OPAL B2
retirement *(n.)* 🔑 B2
series *(n.)* 🔑 OPAL A2
set up *(v. phr.)* 🔑 B1
spare *(n.)* C1
stock *(n.)* 🔑 OPAL B2
tool *(n.)* 🔑 OPAL A2
tedious *(adj.)* C1
truly *(adv.)* 🔑 B2
weigh in *(v. phr.)* C2

UNIT 4

affordable *(adj.)* 🔑 B2
alternative *(n.)* 🔑 OPAL A2
astonishing *(adj.)* 🔑 B2
capacity *(n.)* 🔑 OPAL B2
double *(v.)* 🔑 A2
dramatically *(adv.)* 🔑 B2
extent *(n.)* 🔑 OPAL B2
force *(n.)* 🔑 OPAL B1
function *(v.)* 🔑 OPAL B2
gear *(n.)* 🔑 C1
hazardous *(adj.)* C1
hilarious *(adj.)* 🔑 B2
intention *(n.)* 🔑 OPAL B1
inventor *(n.)* B1
noticeable *(adj.)* C1

power *(v.)* 🔑 B2
rapidly *(adv.)* 🔑 OPAL B2
reflect *(v.)* 🔑 OPAL B1
sophisticated *(adj.)* 🔑 B2
stream *(v.)* C1
summarize *(v.)* 🔑 OPAL B1
target *(n.)* 🔑 OPAL A2
throughout *(prep.)* 🔑 OPAL B1

UNIT 5

alter *(v.)* 🔑 OPAL B2
buzz *(v.)* C1
compound *(v.)* C1
consumer *(n.)* 🔑 B1
debate *(n.)* 🔑 OPAL B2
distribute *(v.)* 🔑 OPAL B2
disturbing *(adj.)* 🔑 C1
dominate *(v.)* 🔑 OPAL B2
ethics *(n.)* 🔑 OPAL B2
ignorance *(n.)* 🔑 C1
infection *(n.)* 🔑 B2
intense *(adj.)* 🔑 B2
load *(n.)* 🔑 B2
modification *(n.)* 🔑 C1
precision *(n.)* 🔑 OPAL C1
productivity *(n.)* 🔑 C1
reaction *(n.)* 🔑 OPAL B1
revolution *(n.)* 🔑 B2
suffer *(v.)* 🔑 B1
survey *(n.)* 🔑 OPAL A2
ultimate *(adj.)* 🔑 OPAL B2

UNIT 6

altogether *(adv.)* 🔑 B2
basically *(adv.)* 🔑 OPAL B2
burst *(v.)* 🔑 C1
confidence *(n.)* 🔑 B2
decent *(adj.)* 🔑 B2
disposable *(adj.)* C1
expand *(v.)* 🔑 OPAL B1
fairness *(n.)* 🔑 C1

fierce *(adj.)* 🔑 C1
genius *(n.)* 🔑 B2
in particular *(idm.)* 🔑 OPAL B1
investor *(n.)* 🔑 B2
launch *(v.)* 🔑 B2
massive *(adj.)* 🔑 B2
meaningful *(adj.)* 🔑 OPAL C1
miserable *(adj.)* 🔑 B2
predecessor *(n.)* 🔑 C1
pressure *(n.)* 🔑 OPAL B1
profit *(n.)* 🔑 B1
rate *(n.)* 🔑 OPAL A2
steadily *(adv.)* 🔑 B2
values *(n.)* 🔑 OPAL B1
vision *(n.)* 🔑 B2
workforce *(n.)* 🔑 B2

UNIT 7

ache *(v.)* A2
adhesive *(n.)* C2
adopt *(v.)* 🔑 OPAL B2
alert *(adj.)* 🔑 C1
biological *(adj.)* 🔑 B2
deprived *(adj.)* C1
exploit *(v.)* 🔑 OPAL B2
face to face *(adv. phr.)* C1
flammable *(adj.)* C2
inadvertent *(adj.)* C2
in all probability *(adv. phr.)* C1
inconceivable *(adj.)* C2
interact *(v.)* 🔑 OPAL B2
mandatory *(adj.)* 🔑 C1
obvious *(adj.)* 🔑 OPAL B1
odds *(n.)* 🔑 C1
reunion *(n.)* C1
synthetic *(adj.)* C1
unreliable *(adj.)* B1
vastly *(adv.)* B2

UNIT 8

abstract *(adj.)* 🔑 B2
cater to *(v. phr.)* C1
dependency *(n.)* C1
dive into *(v. phr.)* C2
diversity *(n.)* 🔑 OPAL B2
engagement *(n.)* 🔑 C1
entirely *(adv.)* 🔑 OPAL B2
fulfilled *(adj.)* B2
generic *(adj.)* 🔑 C1
gut *(n.)* 🔑 C1
harm *(n.)* 🔑 OPAL B2
idle *(adj.)* C1
intimate *(adj.)* 🔑 C1
loosely *(adv.)* C1
manual *(adj.)* C1
necessarily *(adv.)* 🔑 OPAL B1
notion *(n.)* 🔑 OPAL B2
outcome *(n.)* 🔑 OPAL B2
philosophical *(adj.)* 🔑 C1
prospective *(adj.)* 🔑 C1
subtle *(adj.)* 🔑 C1
theoretically *(adv.)* OPAL C1
uniformity *(n.)* C2

AUTHORS AND CONSULTANTS

AUTHORS

Robert Freire holds an M.A. in Applied Linguistics from Montclair State University in New Jersey. He is a teacher and materials developer with more than ten years of ELT experience. He most recently taught ESL and linguistics at Montclair State University.

Tamara Jones holds a Ph.D. in Education from the University of Sheffield in the United Kingdom. She has taught in Russia, Korea, the United Kingdom, Belgium, and the United States. She is currently the Associate Director of the English Language Center at Howard Community College in Maryland. She specializes in the areas of pronunciation and conversation.

SERIES CONSULTANTS

Lawrence J. Zwier holds an M.A. in TESL from the University of Minnesota. He is currently the Associate Director for Curriculum Development at the English Language Center at Michigan State University in East Lansing. He has taught ESL/EFL in the United States, Saudi Arabia, Malaysia, Japan, and Singapore.

Marguerite Ann Snow holds a Ph.D. in Applied Linguistics from UCLA. She teaches in the TESOL M.A. program in the Charter College of Education at California State University, Los Angeles. She was a Fulbright scholar in Hong Kong and Cyprus. In 2006, she received the President's Distinguished Professor award at CSULA. She has trained ESL teachers in the United States and EFL teachers in more than 25 countries. She is the author/editor of numerous publications in the areas of content-based instruction, English for academic purposes, and standards for English teaching and learning. She is a co-editor of *Teaching English as a Second or Foreign Language* (4th ed.).

CRITICAL THINKING CONSULTANT James Dunn is a Junior Associate Professor at Tokai University and the Coordinator of the JALT Critical Thinking Special Interest Group. His research interests include critical thinking skills' impact on student brain function during English learning as measured by EEG. His educational goals are to help students understand that they are capable of more than they might think and to expand their cultural competence with critical thinking and higher-order thinking skills.

ASSESSMENT CONSULTANT Elaine Boyd has worked in assessment for over 30 years for international testing organizations. She has designed and delivered courses in assessment literacy and is also the author of several EL exam coursebooks for leading publishers. She is an Associate Tutor (M.A. TESOL/Linguistics) at University College, London. Her research interests are classroom assessment, issues in managing feedback, and intercultural competences.

VOCABULARY CONSULTANT Cheryl Boyd Zimmerman is Professor Emeritus at California State University, Fullerton. She specialized in second-language vocabulary acquisition, an area in which she is widely published. She taught graduate courses on second-language acquisition, culture, vocabulary, and the fundamentals of TESOL, and has been a frequent invited speaker on topics related to vocabulary teaching and learning. She is the author of *Word Knowledge: A Vocabulary Teacher's Handbook* and Series Director of *Inside Reading, Inside Writing*, and *Inside Listening and Speaking*, published by Oxford University Press.

ONLINE INTEGRATION Chantal Hemmi holds an Ed.D. TEFL and is a Japan-based teacher trainer and curriculum designer. Since leaving her position as Academic Director of the British Council in Tokyo, she has been teaching at the Center for Language Education and Research at Sophia University in an EAP/CLIL program offered for undergraduates. She delivers lectures and teacher trainings throughout Japan, Indonesia, and Malaysia.

COMMUNICATIVE GRAMMAR CONSULTANT Nancy Schoenfeld holds an M.A. in TESOL from Biola University in La Mirada, California, and has been an English language instructor since 2000. She has taught ESL in California and Hawaii, and EFL in Thailand and Kuwait. She has also trained teachers in the United States and Indonesia. Her interests include teaching vocabulary, extensive reading, and student motivation. She is currently an English Language Instructor at Kuwait University.